To my Lanconte
cousi

THE CAPE
CRUSADERS

BY
JULIAN WALKER

www.julianwalker.info
www.thecapecrusaders.com
www.capetocape87.com

Grosvenor House
Publishing Limited

This book is published by
Grosvenor House Publishing Ltd
28-30 High Street, Guildford, Surrey, GU1 3EL.
www.grosvenorhousepublishing.co.uk

A CIP record for this book
is available from the British Library

ISBN 978-1-78148-663-4

For Wendy, Maya and Lucas - my wonderful, loving and supportive family.

Contents

Foreword

In the pre-internet, pre-mobile phone days of the late 1980s, travelling through remote countries with no form of contact back home except for a local Post Office, or the occasional pay phone was the norm.

Not only that, it was completely accepted as the norm back home, so the prospect of facing challenges on the road, with a team of friends added to the bonding experience and camaraderie on the trip.

It also created a unity with fellow travellers, which is nowadays sometimes lost in the enthusiasm to blog or post experiences for the world to share instantaneously.

The speed with which technology has advanced should be embraced (and I would certainly have benefitted from GPS on other expeditions and trips in Africa and South America), but I can't help feeling that some of the achievements of the Cape-to-Cape expedition may not have been so memorable for me, at least, had we emblazoned every minute on the internet.

Having said that, some twenty five-plus years after the event, I have posted some stills from video we shot on the expedition for wider viewing of our experiences and these can be found on www.flickr.com, www.facebook.com and www.pinterest.com, and more information can be found on my website www.julianwalker.info.

Prologue

"Money! Give us some money! Now!" said the two scruffily dressed gunmen.

The gun barrels, levelled at our chests, bobbed in time with the sound of their laughter, which sounded menacing in the still-night air.

Here we were in Africa at one o'clock in the morning on a piece of moonlit ground right next to a railway line, with two armed men, seemingly intent on violent robbery at the very least. My heart was pounding and my sweat went cold on my skin. They had already taken our passports and now Wink and I scrabbled in our pockets for whatever money we had. My mind frantically raced through the options but came up blank. I mentally added up the total collection of coins and crumpled notes - almost £5. "We're dead" I thought.

The train tracks rumbled faintly as a train approached in the distance and I held the money out to the man nearest me. He snatched the money, crumpled it up in his fist and said something to his colleague and gestured with his gun. "Go! You go – now!"

The expectation of feeling bullets rip through my back rose like a growing spectre over my shoulder with every step back over the railway and across the scrubland. We stumbled over a foul smelling drainage ditch and into safety of our hotel compound. It was like wading through marshmallow and my feet felt so heavy and slow. When I eventually stole a fleeting glimpse over my shoulder as we reached safety, I realised that our two assailants were long gone.

So much for the value of life: £2.50 per head. Some who know me may not agree, but there is no doubt in my mind – it is still the best value for money I have ever experienced.

* * *

Principal Players

Expedition Team

Carey 'Wink' Ogilvie (*Expedition Accountant*) – an adventurous, entrepreneurial Scot, fervently convinced that there was more to life than the thrills and spills of being a London estate agent.

Charles Norwood (*Expedition Leader*) – a vastly experienced overland travel professional, expedition leader and excellent photographer. Having led parties of adventure tourists throughout Africa for many years in sensible Bedford trucks for adventure travel group, Encounter Overland, he said he was naturally drawn to the prospect of trying an overland trip in an old fire engine, which was patently not suited to the job.

Chelsea 'Ched' Renton (*Expedition Diarist and Videographer*) – a hugely talented and creative artist, with a wicked sense of humour and keen wit. Ched was a natural for recording events in writing and film (both on video and as stand-in camera man for when the film crew were not with us).

Gerry Moffatt (*Deputy Expedition Leader*) – our other vastly experienced overland travel professional, expedition leader, rafting guide, kayaker and all round adventurer, with an inexhaustible supply of anecdotes and stories.

Jamie Lewis (*Expedition Mechanic*) – a highly prolific and successful yachtsman, looking to broaden his horizons from that of the London marine insurance market, Jamie was also keen to experience the world on dry land and have a crack at a more mechanical side to life.

Jim Everett (Expedition *Navigator*) – also a highly proficient ocean going yachtsman, medical man and ardent tea drinker, Jim was nominally in charge of the Land Rover (which he christened Eric) and was definitely keen to sample the delights of steeping his favourite brew in obscure destinations.

Julian Walker (*Expedition Supplies*) – a well-travelled backpacker and Lloyds Insurance Broker looking to have a completely different CV experience to mask a lack of educational qualifications.

Team back in London (main protagonists only)

Alex da Silva – without her ability to turn a *no* into a *yes*, I am sure that the whole project would have been considerably less successful.

David Henriques (*Cape-to-Cape '87 Chairman*) – a cracking enthusiast for all things and a practical problem solver, David not only kept the momentum of the Cape-to-Cape on track, but he also managed to keep his insurance broking employers happy despite seeming (to me at least) to be spending every waking moment on the project. He is also the only man I could think of who would take the capsizing of his prized boat on dry land (by me) with a casual wave, smile and search for the tow rope to right it.

John Dennis – eponymous hero of the red fire engine (the only true vehicle to associate with the fire brigade). His twinkling blue eyes and sense of mischief belied an ability to get things done efficiently, on time and in budget, and a man who took the proposal of what we wanted to do with one of his vehicles, completely in his stride as if this was perfectly normal.

Luli Thompson – she brought more tireless energy to the party than the cartoon character, Billy Whizz on speed, and kept on driving things forward.

Paul Calkin (*Cape-to-Cape '87 Finance Director*) – a fabulously confident individual who epitomised Kipling's man and applied his sense of humour and business acumen to ensuring that, despite everyone's best endeavours, the project kept on track, was financially stable and delivered its goals.

Warren Burton (*Expedition Training Instructor*) – a highly seasoned Encounter Overland operative, whose wise counsel, expertise and insights during training weekends and in preparation for the expedition stood us in good stead throughout the trip.

Film Team

Graham Smith (Director/Cameraman) – highly creative and skilled at his profession who by the end of the expedition was equally adept stripping his Aaton camera down, cleaning it and putting it back together again blindfolded.

John Keedwell (Assistant Director/Cameraman) – together with Tim on sound, managed to bring out the silly side in all of us, even when we were being serious.

Tim Fraser (Sound Recordist) – possibly the first and only man to erect a self-designed tent on a moving Land Rover, using a sound pole, grips and tarpaulin and the talk his way into riding in the fire engine.

Vikki Norwood (Producer) – almost always smiling and, despite having to deal with almost insurmountable budget issues, her film of the expedition, *Life Calls*,* really captured its essence and is a testament to her ambition and the skill of the people she brought to it to make it happen.

Life Calls was I believe screened on TV in various countries after the event but is sadly languishing in some video vault at present.

CHAPTER 1

Plans – preparation – departure

The air in London was light and breezy that night and the conversation around the dinner table took its cue from there. We flitted from subject to subject until David seemed to engage most of the table with a tale of cancelled plans for a vintage car rally through Africa. "It is a shame it's not going ahead," he mused. "Can you imagine what it would have been like?"

"But what's to stop you doing it anyway David?" said someone. "You could still go off in the car with a friend."

"Yes," said someone else, grasping at the idea enthusiastically. "You could do it as a fund-raising exercise and raise money along the way. You would need an eye-catching vehicle to attract people's attention. I mean, think of the potential."

"Instead of a car, what about taking a wildly-painted camper van?"

"Too Australian."

"Or a London double-decker bus?"

"Too Cliff Richard – no thanks."

"How about a fire engine? That would be really impressive. And, you wouldn't have to stop for water in the desert."

Several other ideas were thrown into the pot but David was already scheming.

"I think John Dennis, who makes Dennis fire engines is an old boy from my school," he said on the steps of the house as we were leaving. "Perhaps I could ring him and see if he has a fire engine we could maybe borrow. It is a strange enough request, and if he doesn't, well, at least we tried. What do you think?"

Showing a surprisingly casual disregard for conformity, Paul Calkin agreed. "Nothing to lose then David, why not?"

"Give me 24 hours and if I can find a suitable one, then it's yours, David. I'll be in touch," said John Dennis and was as good as his word within only 12 hours. "I've found you a fourteen-year-old one that Devon Fire and Rescue say you can borrow," he said.

And that was John. From the moment that David spoke to him we realised that we had to go ahead. Until I met him, I thought that enthusiasm would be limited for a hair-brained scheme such as driving a fire engine from within the Arctic Circle down to the southern tip of

Africa, but I am pleased that I was wrong. John has one of the most infectious personalities I have ever come across and his enthusiasm for life seemed hugely fitting for the final charity for whom we chose to raise money.

And so it was that, bleary-eyed from an imprudently late finish to the night before, seven people from wildly differing lives, assembled at a rather unassuming looking terraced house in South West London at the beginning of November 1987 to set off on what has come to be known as the Cape-to-Cape '87 expedition.

We were a mixed bunch and most of us unknowing of what lay in store. Charlie Norwood, a tough outdoors professional travel leader for an overland travel tour company called Encounter Overland, was the natural chief for the expedition. Gerry Moffatt, his old friend, Encounter Overland colleague and a professional rafting guide in Nepal, was his deputy. Our navigator, Jim Everett, was a child psychologist from Reading by day and successful ocean yachtsman whenever possible and our diarist was Chelsea 'Ched' Renton, an artist and graphic designer. They all put their work on hold for the duration of the trip.

Carey 'Wink' Ogilvie, a fellow Scot like Gerry, had cast aside the life of a London estate agent, while Jamie Lewis and I had left the security of our City jobs as Lloyd's insurance brokers.

***

The exhausts from the red Dennis F108, manual transmission fire engine powered by a Perkins V8 diesel engine, which was parked outside the railings - effectively blocking the narrow Pimlico residential street, had sounded shocking and offensively deafening in the still of the Monday morning. However, as my prospective home for the next three and a half months, it seemed reassuring solid and friendly in its presence.

It was two and a half years since I had drunkenly agreed to become involved in the bizarre – some might say mad-cap – scheme to drive a fire engine from Nord Cap, the northernmost tip of Europe, to Cape Agulhas, the southernmost extremity of Africa; and, only a few months since I had been selected to actually go on the trip itself, so I was still unsure as to what I should expect.

I looked around at my fellow travellers: "Well, this is it," I thought. "I hope they know what they are doing, because I sure as hell don't."

We had spent the previous seven days frantically shopping for last minute items and packing for the three month journey ahead. Everything was now carefully stored in the 14-year-old fire engine and in the spankingly new long-wheel base Land Rover County – which had also been lent to us for our odyssey by its makers.

Allegedly I was in charge of supplies – but thankfully Charlie, and his operational boss at Encounter Overland in London, Warren Burton, had done a very thorough job on preparing the lists. Food, spare parts, fuel, clothing, camping equipment, medical kit – all the requirements – had been meticulously reviewed and checked off. Nothing was to be left to chance and more importantly, from the perspective of everyone on the trip, nothing was to be left too much to my control, as my own tastes and ideas are somewhat eclectic.

Apart from being absolutely knackered by the time we set off, several of us had the sort of colds that really slow down your thinking process, and so everything was checked and double checked. Also, before setting off for the real start to the trip we engaged in a round of media interviews to publicise our fundraising cause and the journey itself. Since the trip I have meandered into the world of public relations and, although I wouldn't go so far as to credit Charlie's first radio interview on LBC as a career path revelation of Damascene proportions, it was probably my earliest registration of the power of the media (my parents said they had heard the broadcast).

We moved on from LBC's studios to our departure point outside St Stephen's Church, Walbrook and parked the two vehicles creatively for the press photo-call. We spent the early part of the morning, jumping on and off the vehicles brandishing garishly coloured golfing umbrellas from one of our sponsors, to the flashes, clicks and whirrs of the assembled press photographers. The man from The Times was more selective in his choice of picture and the next day they ran a small picture of HRH Duchess of Kent quizzically holding up my lunch, a chicken drumstick, which she had found hidden behind the fire engine's winch where I had put it in a vain attempt to show some decorum when faced with dignitaries.

We had chosen to launch the trip from St Stephen's as the crypt was where the Reverend Prebendary

Chad Varah had founded and initially operated The Samaritans – the object of all fundraising surrounding the expedition itself. The launch date was also almost 35 years since he had begun the organisation and we were extremely privileged to have him there to see us off. Despite a long career working with countless people, he is without doubt one of the most extraordinarily inspirational people I have ever met.

The send-off was like a dream as we pulled out of the courtyard, to a highly illegal quick burst of our sirens and, with flashing blue lights and hazards ablaze, we drove sedately down Queen Victoria Street in convoy. We were preceded by 40 members of the Devon Fire and Rescue Band and a group of people who were running in the London Marathon to raise funds for the Samaritans. It was a surprisingly moving experience and one that hastened us on to a new and exciting challenge.

We parted company with the band on Blackfriars Bridge over London's river Thames – a bridge made infamous for the mysterious death of "God's Banker", Roberto Calvi some years earlier who had been found hanging underneath it one morning after the collapse of his employer Banco Ambrosiano in suspicious circumstances. And from there we were off to our first night on the road – a pub with no name at Easthorpe in Essex – in the thickest fog I can remember.

"The trick to driving in fog," said Jim wisely to me, with his pipe firmly clenched in his teeth for extra scholarly effect, (after we had not only managed to lose the other vehicle in the zero visibility, but also the pub and the village,) "is to let someone overtake you and then stick to their rear lights like glue." We assiduously followed this tip every time an Essex boy racer overtook us and did eventually find our goal and the rest of the team, but I couldn't help wondering if my map reading needed to be a bit better in the Sahara.

The next morning the fog was gone, but the grey cold remained as we drove onto the ferry in the Essex port of Harwich and headed for the continental port of the Hook of Holland, from where an overnight drive to Friedrichshaven in northern Germany awaited us. On board the ferry we experienced the first of many curious entertainments we would experience along the way, and as Gerry passed verdict on the ship's cabaret, we fervently hoped that this would be the low point.

"I reckon," he said loudly during a particularly dire and achingly silent pause in the on stage comedy routine, "that this might be used as a training ground for NASA astronauts needing to acclimatise to a place with no atmosphere."

CHAPTER 2

Off the blocks and up to the starting line

Our first real glimpse of continental Europe was of a very flat landscape which whisked past with hardly any discernable features of interest. The border crossings were more interesting than usual being as we were in an emergency vehicle, but only the Danish officials insisted on us taping over our blue lights whilst in their country.

Having engaged in what seemed like an overly long discussion about this with the female border guard, Charlie swung himself back up into the cab and lustily informed us that he was "in lurve."

"It's a uniform thing," said Gerry. "It'll happen again and it won't last," he predicted and was right on both counts.

The taping over of the lights proved to have been an amateur job by us and was short-lived, but at least we had begun the more adventurous element of our journey and, after another brief ferry crossing, we set up rough camp 30 kilometres along the E4 out of Gothenburg.

And what a campsite it was, amongst the pine cones, rocks and road kill – and all this only a hair's breadth from the edge of the motorway. Our tent pitching proved to be almost as inadequate and only marginally better than our light taping over, and before long we had bent most of the tent pegs trying to anchor the flysheets into the frozen ground, whipped up a meal of rehydrated stew powder and experienced an all too short night under canvas. All too soon it was the crack of dawn and time to begin the four day drive north to Hammerfest to catch yet another ferry to the Island of Nord Cap. This was our first goal, the northern most point of Europe and was the real starting point of the Cape-to-Cape.

The light was still insipid and barely recognisable as day when we had our first worry – the radiator on the fire engine had become somewhat dysfunctional. Despite being a state of mind to which we could all relate at that time in the morning, it was a situation which gained little sympathy and so we let Charlie tinker with it. We had a limited time schedule and needed to average 350 miles per day for this stretch to cover the 2,500-kilometre trek northwards and, whilst warmth would be a key requirement, we needed it to be controllable under the engine hood.

As the trip went on, I was to learn that tinkering was one of the many technical terms I would pick up from Charlie. Buggered was another technical term I was soon to learn from Charlie, but for the time being I was unaware of this and was quietly impressed when he got back in the cab and we set off. Within minutes the indicator lights come out in sympathy with the radiator and provided an erratic disco display of attention seeking.

* * *

"Routine is one of the ways that expeditions run smoothly," said Gerry authoritatively, "and so we are dividing up into teams for the next few days." Charlie, Gerry, Jamie and I were now in the fire engine, while Wink, Ched and Jim travelled in the Land Rover. I don't think that sexism entered into it and we were a few years too early for laddism, but the arrangement seemed to work well – for the first couple of days at least.

Radiator and indicator lights aside, we made good time and pitched camp in Ronan, near Gavle, the oldest city in Norland (Sweden's Northern Lands) mainly known for its Grevalia coffee. It had been a surprisingly tiring day and, despite the coffee, we were in our sleeping bags and asleep before even thinking of missing the Guy Fawkes fireworks back home.

Driving a large vehicle on motorways through flat countryside was not an overly inspiring experience, even when the vehicle is as exciting as a fire engine. It did, however, provide us with time, the first in months, to sit and think about what we were doing and to settle into the routine of who sat in which seat, who drove after whom and who did what when we stopped.

All very mundane, you might think, but these things seem to matter rather a lot when you are facing the prospect of spending more time with these six people over the next three and a half months, than you would spend sitting next to a work colleague for ten years. We were beginning to get to know each other's characters and personalities – and most importantly their senses of humour.

I remember thinking that, at last, I would have a chance to find out what it was that I really wanted to do with my life and drifted off into a reverie – what would I do? How would I do it? Would it be cool? Yes, very cool, in fact ... icy...

... I surfaced from my musings to an acute awareness that the cold, icy wind was coming through from somewhere. I put myself to work sourcing the blast as it meant that there was a dangerous gap somewhere in the cab and it needed sealing. I soon realised that it wasn't a draft, merely that leaning my leg against the metal part of the door wasn't overly bright in near freezing conditions, I contented myself by looking out at the localised snow storms as we drove past and imagined the chill. More than can be said for the radiator, which under the worsening conditions, began to heat up alarmingly.

By the time we reached the university town of Umea, Charlie was sufficiently concerned about the radiator to stop for a cup of tea – a euphemism for calling John Dennis for a bit of advice – but, after a little long distance tele-tinkering we then decided to camp somewhere for the night. This took several hours. However, we eventually found a formal campsite and sparsely populated town called Lovanger, in county of Vasterbotten (which I misheard and so greatly amused me, not least because I'd never stayed in an enormous bottom before). While Charlie and Jamie replaced one of the thermostats in the fire engine, the rest of us cooked supper and set up camp, as, being made of hardy stuff, camping in the freezing cold now held no terrors for any of us.

While we wrestled with freezing winds, errant fly sheets and tent pegs – already contorted into Gordian Knots from our earlier attempts at hammering them into frozen ground and so not especially useful – a figure materialised from out of the gloom.

"Check out the loos, guys," said Gerry. "There's hot showers, heating and no drafts. I'm for sleeping in there as there's no-one else in this place."

And so it was that, despite being made of hardy stuff, we dismantled the tents and within record time were re-installed inside the men's washroom, enjoying hot showers, clean hair and too many tots of whisky. Gerry and Ched showed great adeptness at hairdressing – cutting the knots from Wink's mane and even managing to make it four inches shorter in some places – while everyone played up for the video camera, badly singing songs and melodramatically avoiding being caught on film while using the loos for their intended purpose.

The next morning we took exact directions to our bog standard hotel for the return journey, and I am glad that we proved more adept at navigating in Africa – as we never even found the right road on the way back.

***

Whenever I have to get up early I am always reminded of the silly saying "To bed with the lark and up with the cock." Pathetic though the humour is, it usually makes me smile, but I was beginning to wonder what drove everyone else to be up at those small hours.

Under the cover of a weak and pale sunrise, we came across a bizarre fellow who was apparently a seal spotter, but to Wink's eye he resembled a KGB spy. We could see no such mammals, but then he had some enormous binoculars around his neck, so who were we to argue with Rudolf (as we thought he had introduced himself). He was very affable for that time in the morning and, despite being wrapped up in enough clothing for him to have lost most of his human shape, he was very animated and insisted we take a side road and cut through Finland in our Northern quest. At least that's what we thought, but his voice was so muffled and inaudible through his layers of clothing that he might well have told us to turn around and give up.

"It saves us about 200 kilometres," said Jamie cheerily from the depths of his own hood and looking up from a guide book. "And we might even get to see some reindeer."

And we did just that.

Around every bend they were strolling across the road, standing and even lying down and blocking the road (presumably in protest at the weather). So, Jamie was right but our communist friend was wrong about predicting wet weather – which didn't stop Ched's excruciating pun when she turned from speaking to him: "Rudolf the Red knows rain dear."

Perhaps he had a sense of humour though, as Finland's icy roads proved more than a match for a sedate 14-year-old fire engine. In fact we had to face it, when it came to driving on snow and ice, we were amateurs. As the day wore one, we were constantly overtaken by disgusted Fins who amply displayed their feelings for a 30 mph speed limit (and our own sedate progress), despite the cold winds. Our windows remained tightly up and the only hand gestures we did were stretching fingers inside our gloves.

When travelling, it is funny how things take on a sense of proportion that is wholly divorced from their normal bent and even winning a children's game can be intensely satisfying. One evening on the route to the Baltic in a tiny Swiss-style chalet 20 kilometres south of Sodankyla (once again we had taken hot water and warmth over canvas in the snow), we were having a marathon game of the board game Ludo, when Wink and Ched just about gave the game to Jim. Jamie was disgusted but Jim leant back smiling, languidly removed his pipe and uttered his favourite word. A very long, slow and contented won-der-ful.

My diary from these days is fairly repetitive – snow and ice, ice and snow and snow-ice. Perfect conditions for playing games and thinking long thoughts, however, we kept our spirits up and soon crossed into Norway, having narrowly missed a wrong turn into the Soviet Union at Ivalo, complete with a signpost to Murmansk. We were at least able to experience the area's famous sense of humour in the stony faced reaction from the Norwegian/Finnish border guards at my reply of "Finland" to their first question:

"And where have you come from?"

Revisiting this joke some twenty-five years after its nativity, I am not sure that they were altogether wrong in their response and that perhaps the witticism should have been put down at birth. On the other hand, I have told many a worse joke since then and I am glad to say I am none the worse for this early setback to a career in comedy. Some years before the trip I had in fact tried a stand-up comedy routine in front of around 250 people and their reception should have prepared me better for the reactions of the Norwegian border guard.

In any event, we passed safely through the border and celebrated that evening with that classic winter warmer – Southern Comfort (already small victories and life on the road were beginning to take their toll on our sanity).

Maybe it was the Southern Comfort influence, or maybe some repressed desire from a bygone era, but that night Gerry revisited thoughts of being a hairdresser, this time with Jamie and I as his slightly unwilling models. Anyhow, two spiky haircuts later (and the curious discovery that there used to be a hairdressing salon in

Southend-on-Sea in Essex called 'Beau Locks'), Gerry relaxed, satisfied with his evening's work and, having fallen asleep in his moussaka, fell prey to Jamie's own version of Sweeney Todd, and lost his moustache to a strangely blunt razor. Despite having proved to be curiously during our meal, the moussaka at least provided the necessary lather for shaving.

During all of this Jim alternatively sang, grumbled and wonderfulled contentedly in the corner, extolling the virtues of pipe smoking and the life aquatic – his passion being big yacht sailing. I wasn't much help in this conversation as, in spite of David Henriques' attempts to teach me to sail back home, I had never got my head around the concept of going from left to right and back again when a motor boat could get you somewhere in a straight line.

After a week on the road there was great excitement the next morning (except from Gerry who constantly complained about the coldness of his upper lip) in that the weather deteriorated to minus 12°C – cold enough to warrant chains on the tyres. Now, putting chains on a normal car tyre is not something everyone has done, I grant you, but fitting them over tyres on a fire engine which were over a meter in diameter, was even more complicated. To further prove a point on the temperature, and Gerry's facial nudity, the sea had actually started to freeze and waves were weighed down and sluggish as if made from thick, dark treacle with icing sugar on top. Having put the chains on the tyres and stared at the rapidly solidifying sea, my own enthusiasm for the previous evening's trimming abated as my ears went blue and the scalped sides of my head took on the consistency of a frozen chicken (with a short stubble covering, if such a thing were possible).

As we drove into the port town of Hammerfest, I was strangely delighted to discover its naming origins – after 'Hammer', some huge, long gone rocks against which you could 'fest', or fasten your boat. Not perhaps fascinating, but as I say, it amused me. And this was an emotion curiously absent among the film crew when we met up with them in town, as they saw our ridiculous haircuts. Graham, our director and chief cameraman, wandered about morosely muttering something that sounded like "that's the continuity plucked then."

They did however arrange for some great accommodation for us – the floor of the Hammerfest Hotel's conference room – which while hard and cluttered with desks, was at least warm and not for one moment did we envy the film crew's budget, luxury rooms or soft beds in the nearby Hotel Rica.

But Hammerfest was the launch pad for the last leg of the journey north to our starting point, the island of Nordkapp – the northernmost tip of Europe – and a little more discomfort was not going to spoil our mood.

***

Sponsors for any trip such as ours are all important, and without their generosity many expeditions would founder. I remember being told by a travel journalist at the time that there are in the region of a hundred charitable expeditions proposed each year to the major charities in the UK, and of these, approximately three get off the drawing board and one every other year is successful. These are statistics and as everyone knows, there are 'lies, damn lies and statistics' but they made the point to us and that was what counted and we remained eternally grateful to all those who helped us along the way.

Anyway, apart from eating the tinfoil packed boil-in the bag meals we were testing for a company called General Foods and all the equipment we used without immediately mentally thanking the donor, shipping was the first and most obvious sponsorship support we received.

Fred Olsen Lines, had not only shipped us over to the mainland of Continental Europe, but at Honigsvag, they excelled in providing practical solutions to our unique travel requirements. And so it was that the Land Rover and fire engine came to be unceremoniously hoisted up into the air with the grace of injured hippopotami and lowered into the voluminous hold of the Olsen Lines vessel, Midnatsol. Years later I was reminded of the scene while watching the reluctant cow being lowered into the tyrannosaurus rex enclosure in the Steven Spielberg movie, Jurassic Park. Unlike that experience for the movie characters though, we happily went on to be treated by the purser to a huge breakfast on board – film crew included, which greatly pleased Tim, our sound man, despite cruel asides from his colleagues insinuating that he had already availed himself of the buffet at the Hotel Rica.

We then had the most spectacular journey of breath-taking beauty, looking out across the Arctic and snow-covered islands through air that was so clear and clean that we couldn't work out why our vision was so sharp. For those who haven't had the pleasure, it is an awesome, and yet slightly unnerving visual experience, and something I re-visited some years later when in Iceland with my now wife, Wendy. Living in a city you do not realise the extent of the air pollution around you which takes the clarity out of your vision.

Maturely, Ched and I got the giggles at the prospect of being invited onto the bridge to fiddle with the Captain's knobs (at least that is what she told me he had said), but the air was so clear and the views so spectacular that we had at least managed some decorum by the time Midnatsol docked in Honigsvag, the port on the southern shore of the isle of Nordkapp. It was just after lunch, although it could just as well have been midnight as the light was so dim that the snow covered surroundings had a deathly subdued feeling about them, but we were cheered by the kind provision of free rooms each by the North Cape Hotel. Ched and I decided to wash the fire engine in preparation for filming the next day. This was an almost impossible task, as the hot water froze within seconds of contact with the freezing metal sides of the vehicle. Still, it did look shiny and as Wink pointed out, it was the thought that counted.

To prove to the film crew that we had been getting some footage in the can for them whilst they were not with us, we asked reception to screen our video coverage in Charlie's room. There was some confusion caused by the language barrier and also the nature of our request, but the task was soon accomplished. However, we were unaware until breakfast the following day that the film had in fact been screened to all and sundry on the hotel only working TV/video channel. We got some funny looks over the eggs and bacon and, whether it was the filming in the men's loo at Lovanger, or the fact that the other guests wondered if we were subversive film stars, I don't know, but we had a good laugh about it on the road.

Leaving the adoring glances of our star-struck fans behind us, we set off for the last northward part of our journey so that we could, at last, begin the journey south.

The drive to the northernmost point of Europe was much easier than we had expected, the roads being reasonably clear. Sadly this was not because of the cultural and geographical interest of the point, but because there was a hotel being constructed on the site and our fire engine was probably the smallest vehicle to have driven the route in the past twelve months.

Today I gather, visitors can enjoy the metal-ribbed globe which marks the northernmost point in Europe from the comfort of a midnight sun lounge in the new hotel on site. Back then there was nothing around as we drove up and climbed into it for a closer look. I was either too large, or not athletic enough, to get in with everyone else – my memory plays tricks on me sometimes – but I like to think that the world just wasn't big enough for me as well as the rest of the team.

We had an abortive attempt at a celebratory brunch outside in the snow, but ended up cooking inside the fire engine with the boil-in-the-bags being heated over small gas rings as, at minus 15°C, everything had frozen including the gas canisters. On reflection, this was probably the most dangerous thing we had done so far on the trip, as using naked flames in a confined space or a vehicle cabin, surrounded by flammable materials and too many people could have proved fatal. However, there were no mishaps and we were back at the North Cape Hotel by 3pm, by which time it was already pitch dark so the obviously solution was a mass sauna followed by a frenetic session of disorderly dancing in the hotel disco. At some point in the evening Gerry cracked a tooth, which would develop into an abscess and provide us with the first of several medical emergencies along the way, but for now, we had a common purpose and were happy in our lack of dance co-ordination.

We had successfully reached the first of our two goals and the expedition was on time, on budget and really happening.

* * *

We rose early and left the hotel before most guests were awake. I have always been a morning person, but it is strange that, as a team, we had developed a passion for starting the days at the crack of dawn – probably to get in training for the warmer climes of Africa. In any event, there would be more sunlight further south, of that we were assured.

We fortified ourselves with a huge breakfast at the hotel and arrived at Hammerfest to load on to the ferry. The Captain lowered the film crew off in a smaller boat and then amazingly turned the ferry around and re-entered the harbour – all for the sake of our film. He was an incredibly kind man who only briefly appeared in the final version of the documentary, but probably earned a more lasting impact on his employment record as I am sure that causing wanton delays were not part of his job description.

Having made the crossing safely and after bank and diesel delays, we all set off for another night in Karasjok. Stopping at petrol stations was a long affair as filling up the special tanks we had installed in the fire engine was an unnaturally slow process. And the looks we got from attendants was rather like the old TV prank when a small car with normal fuel capacity, but whose boot and back seat had been secretly converted into a huge petrol tank, is driven for a fill up. As the total goes up, the bemused attendant checks the nozzle, then the gauge, then looks under the car to see if there is a leak, then checks the gauge and nozzle again and then looks around helplessly as the fuel continues to fill the car.

On the road, blizzards like clouds of dry ice, slowed us down considerably and we all sat crammed into vehicles rubbing each other's hands and feet as the temperature dropped rapidly to around minus 25°C, giving a wind-chill factor through the unfixed holes in the fire engine of about minus 40°C.

The blizzards eventually gave way to the most incredible hoar frost, which you could see falling like showers of silver glitter. When we stopped, it also had the unpleasant effect of freezing the hair on the inside of your nose when you breathed in, giving the impression of being instantly and completely blocked up. Sadly, when we arrived at Karasjok the hut we were allocated was absolutely freezing inside, as someone had left the window open and the heating was not working. Still, despite the chill and half-way through a hasty supper (clumsily being eaten whilst fully kitted out in puffa jackets, scarves, hats and ski gloves), a really weird flickering light tempted some of us outside again.

It was the first time that most of us had ever seen the Aurora Borealis, or Northern Lights as they are better known, and despite being lucky enough to now have seen this strange phenomenon several times, it still remains one of the most beautiful sights I have ever seen.

Named after the Roman goddess of the dawn, *Aurora*, and *Boreal*, the Latin word for north, folklore associates the pulsating colours with magic, spirits of the dead, blood draining from the clouds and gods. However, looking in my diary for that night, I note that I was inspired to try to capture the wonder in some fairly poncey terms:

"The brilliant phosphorescence flickered across a dark starlit sky. A beautiful myriad of pastel greens, blues, pinks and reds eerily silhouetted the surrounding hills as the sky pulsated in strange rhythmic waves. The snow underfoot crunched crisply and the sugar-coated trees echoed back and forth the 'oohs!' and 'aahs! of the expectant travellers. Meanwhile back in the cabin

the boil-in-the-bag chicken curry received its own appreciative chorus from those too hungry or disinterested in the Aurora Borealis, which nature was providing for free, to move outside."

The next morning, both vehicles were frozen solid and we had to light torches made of paper and twigs and use the small Calor gas stoves to assist us in reawakening them by letting the hot air be sucked into the vents on the roof while the heat warmed the engine itself from underneath. Success was slow in coming, but after several hours and about 20 breakfasts' worth of gas later, the engines, diesel, etc. were defrosted sufficiently for the snow-muffled silence of the day to be shattered by the roaring machines, and we set off for the Finnish border.

We stopped for tea at a Finnish tourist centre and, much to our disappointment, Charlie acted like a grown up and refused to even entertain the idea of buying some furry dice for the cab. Bearing in mind that travelling in a huge red fire engine, with sponsors' logos emblazoned on the side and a film crew hanging out of passing car windows as we drove past is not perhaps the most unobtrusive way to move around. The dice may have been less of a distraction than he felt. But he was firm in his choice – "Jules, I don't want to drive around looking like an absolute tit, thanks!"

However, 25 years' later I have still never bought any dice, so I guess they were not all that important in the greater meaning of life. More importantly was that night, which we spent in the comfort of the warm Swiss-style chalet near Sodankyla we has used before, with a seemingly endless hot water supply and luxuriously soft beds.

With no great surprise to anyone, we were on the road the next morning before 7.00a,m, hoping to get to our bog-standard heated loos for the night. We stopped for brunch in a lovely rough parking area, which unfortunately turned out to be in a military zone and so the police unceremoniously shovelled us on mid-sandwich. The eggs and most of the other food in the fire engine lockers being now frozen solid, my job as supplies master had failed us in this culinary experience, so I wasn't that peeved by the police intervention.

After the warmth of that experience, Charlie decided that we should drive through the night in order to get to Gottenburg in time for the reception being arranged by the local group of the Samaritans.

Jamie confirmed my thoughts as we set off and the night enveloped us and we sped south: "I'm not sure we were even on the right road for the bog-standard loos anyway, Jules."

We stopped off in Stockholm in the hope of finding the stickers for one of our last minute sponsors. Curiously, their office apparently knew nothing about the trip, despite one of our fund raisers back home insisting they did – which was a frustrating scene we were to experience again through her contacts. Despite not providing stickers, they wished us well and we returned to the vehicles and promptly got lost in a car park trying to find our way out. "Looking good for the Sahara, then," said Wink slyly.

Having successfully negotiated the car park, we arrived in Gottenberg early that evening, changed in the film crew's hotel and set off to the reception with our host Greta, whom some of us had met earlier in the year whilst fundraising for the trip in York, to meet the local team of more Samaritans. After an evening of sharing our experiences on the trip so far, we slept on the floor of the sitting room at the centre and, not for the first time, did I wonder why the film crew budget incorporated luxury where ours appeared to actively promote frugality.

Still, we benefited from their hotel the next day, lazing around and doing media interviews in between hot baths and watching MTV. Gerry also managed to change the ferry tickets to take us directly to Keil in Germany instead of Friedrichshaven, thereby missing out all of Denmark, so, that evening the film crew and us all boarded another overnight boat and experienced yet another water born catastrophe – the ship's disco was filled with old couples surreally waltzing to Michael Jackson singing BAD. Travel certainly does broaden the mind, but in some circumstances, the mind is just not wide enough to cope.

Another comfy night was spent by one and all on the floor in the ship's lounge until we were rudely awoken by the manic cleaning lady who insisted on running us over with her industrial-sized vacuum cleaner. She may have been singing, or shouting at us – it was hard to tell – but we beat a hasty retreat to the vehicle deck and docked without further incident at Keil. It was a grey and listless morning.

The north German countryside proved uneventful as we sped to our next rendezvous with David's step-brother, Marcus – a pilot stationed at RAF Laarbrook, near Dusseldorf – a most generous and convivial host. Having been billeted in rooms in the mess (with beds and not just carpeted floors) we went into the strictly jacket, ties and shirts dining room for supper. Marcus and his colleagues were true gentlemen and never raised an eyebrow at our jeans and Timberland boots, and we happily enjoyed a raucous evening at 30 pence per pint, and found out that our high jinks were actually relatively low when compared to the day to day life in an RAF mess.

We were allowed to use the RAF base as our camp for the next couple of days whilst making several abortive trips into Dusseldorf to pick up the elusive stickers from our supposed sponsor. Unfortunately it eventually transpired that the oil company concerned had declined to support us from the outset, but that the person helping to fund-raise could bring herself to tell us that for fear of having failed, so we wasted time and effort, when in fact no one would have even raised an eyebrow at the outset. An interesting lesson in people psychology and the pointless sticker hunting did produce one benefit, as we filmed more tracking shots up and down the autobahn for the film crew.

On the team front, just as we had got used to his lopsided smile and hamster like appearance, Gerry decided it was now a safe place to visit the dentist and his abscess was dealt with in relative peace. While we parked the fire engine by the side of the runway and were buzzed by Tornado and Harrier planes "for purely film reasons," said Graham, Gerry was buzzed by a dental drill and returned with a grin almost as big as Graham's, who had seemed more and more excited by the proximity to several million pounds worth of fighter jets than our fire engine.

After a couple of days we left Laarbnick in the pouring rain at 3.30pm having ransacked the NAAFI and duty-free shop and drove back to Dusseldorf airport to drop off the film crew and have a great and unexpected laugh at Charlie's expense. After dropping the guys off he jogged off to make a phone call without realising that there was a solid, clear glass booth round the telephone itself. Sadly, this was not the last time on the trip that the camera was not there to record events, however, I was pleased to record that we drove on through Belgium and into France without further incident and that Charlie seemed none the worse for his Marx Brothers moment.

France is a land famed for its fine food, wine and living, so I am not quite sure how we ended up spending the night inside our vehicles in a truckers' lay by, but we did. It was the least comfortable, or hospitable night of the trip so far.

And the theme continued throughout the next day as we spent it in that most cultural of mecca's – a car park (albeit near the Louvre). This time we had not failed to find the exit, but loitering with intent, while Charlie and Gerry travelled backwards and forwards between our makeshift camp and the Rwandan Embassy to secure our passport visas. However, it being a Friday, the answer was a very clear: *"Non! Ce n'est pas possible, messieurs. C'est le weekend."*

Rather than sample the delights of our car park for the next three days – where incidentally I had improved my French vocabulary no end, as many Parisians did not think a great big fire engine, let alone a British one, should be taking up several spaces meant for *les voitures* – we decided to leave Gerry in Paris and meet up with him later in southern Spain.

The volume of Parisian traffic and the apparent total disregard for human life were tremendous and we ended up playing a form of chicken with the other drivers. This did not help our nerves or Jim's navigation skills, which we again began to question as we ended up going down roads only just wide enough for the fire engine itself. This elicited Gallic fist shakes from café proprietors and some more technical *bon mots* from Charlie. At last, after a couple of very tight squeezes, intermingled with meeting a couple of maniacal and impassive French drivers at crossroads, we emerged from the city like a bather from the end of a water shoot and found open roads and limited need for the brake pedal.

By now, we were quite used to stopping at roadside cafés and picnicking on the hard shoulder. So, the first motorway cafe on the road to Orléans was ideal for tea, before setting off to Tours for another spot of roadside camping. And, nobody even mentioned Jim's map reading skills – at all.

As the auto routes unrolled before us, the call of Africa (or was it sunshine?) became louder and louder and we sped on through the countryside with barely a glance and crossed the Spanish border as night approached. We were obviously not destined to be city folk as we fell foul of the signage and got badly lost in Bilbao. Happily, and without resorting to too many technical terms, we eventually found our way out towards Madrid and, exhausted, finally set up camp at midnight, just north of Miranda de Ebro, in the Province of Burgos.

The next day provided some very impressive Spanish scenery, as we drove down to Madrid and on through the plain to an olive grove some 20 kilometres north of Barlen where we spent the night. Being now the hardened travellers we slept under the stars and didn't complain about the bugs who visited in the night and I was able to ruminate on the many useful technical terms and phrases I'd picked up from Charlie and Jim in particular. Kilometres are only ever referred to as clicks, people who are less than helpful are called dipsticks and my culinary skills are listed in the dictionary under shit.

But as shooting stars fired across the night sky and we drank Spanish beers under the olive trees, I remember thinking "experimental cooking requires an educated palate, but who cares – this is immeasurably better than working for a living."

This reverie continued as we positively ambled into the day, rising late and journeying to the coast via Grenada, stopping for lunch overlooking the sea and a rather grim looking gypsy encampment. From a travelling perspective, we were certainly cleaner, fresher and more enthusiastic about life on the road than the characters we ate beside, but then I supposed that they had been travelling a lifetime on the road already. Anyhow, not to be lead astray by Romany roadside customs, that night we booked into a very British campsite that had had two groups of overland travellers through it in the last ten days and we successfully met up with Gerry and the completed Rwanda visa forms.

Spain was having a good lifestyle effect on us and we rose late for the journey to Algeciras and another freebie, the Guardacorte Hotel, courtesy of another of the trip sponsors. We spent a lazy afternoon booking ferry tickets for Africa and watching Gerry windsurf off the beach at Tarrifa, the southernmost tip of Spain.

We were ready for a whole new continent and a completely unexpected series of developments.

CHAPTER 3

That's Africa babe and the top of the Sahara

We were up early to catch the ferry from Algeciras to Ceuta in Africa – but this time with the excitement of a family going on holiday. However, upon landing on mainland Africa the heavens opened with torrential downpours, so there was only one thing to do – shop for essentials, like sunglasses and beer. Jamie and Ched strolled around – not looking remotely like the Blues Brothers, – and then Gerry and I had to quickly spend the last escudos (the pre-Euro currency of Spain) on a beer. We were alarmed to find that the helpful traffic jam outside had now cleared and that the fire engine and Land Rover had gone when we came out of the bar.

Luckily Ceuta is not that big and we ran through the traffic and caught them up down the road, just before the Moroccan border. We need not have bothered to run as the guards turned our whole party back at the border post – they had not received a telex informing them of our travel plans.

Before we had embarked on the expedition, the UK Foreign Office had provided us with letters of introduction to assist with border crossings. We needed these as many we would cross were likely to be less than welcoming. They proved increasingly useful as the trip progressed, although the Moroccan border was not a crossing where we had anticipated any specific problems. Still, the benefits of proper planning are always evident and so, three hours and several frantic phone calls later, we were back at the border post, where a different guard amazingly found the telex, which had in fact been there all the time.

Charlie turned and quietly explained under his breath: "that's Africa babe!" and so it was to be.

A different pace of life and, in fact, a whole different ball game.

Anyhow, fever pitch enthusiasm from the guards was suddenly instilled as one of them found an empty walkie talkie cover, the contents of which had been lost in Finland by the film crew (honest governor, not us). Despite our protestations, it was enough of a reason to strip the vehicles down in search of the missing radio. So my first real experience of African borders was not the smoothest – at least we got plenty of experience using the dipstick phrase.

Anyone who has ever come up against incomprehensible bureaucracy will know the feeling. It is quite a helpless sensation having everything taken out of bags and lockers, unpacked, inspected and then disregarded in favour of something even more enticing in the next locker. For us, it was something to which we would become accustomed. Talcum powder in Wink's wash bag caused immense excitement, until, having taken the lid off and spilled most of the contents onto the sand, the guard became more excited by a spare fuel switch.

Despite their diligence, the illusive walkie talkie remained so and had still not been found some three hours later. With our provisions and spares all now out of their tightly sand-proof-sealed packaging, and Jamie still patiently explaining to one of the dipsticks "It is Christmas cake....honestly....my mother made it," the guards presumably accepted the lack evidence before them and we were quite suddenly waved through into Morocco.

We left the one remaining walkie talkie at the post for collection by an Encounter Overland trip coming the other way a couple of days later and bundled our stuff back into the vehicles while the guards hurried us along, almost as if the delay was our fault.

"Move on! Move on!" was their cheery farewell.

"And that's Africa babe," I thought as we set off into the unknown, camping just north of a town called Mdiq in a small glade which passed for a campsite, whose owner, Mohammed, entertained us with a pot pipe he had made from plumbing supplies. His stories became less intelligible as the evening wore on, as we all sat on decrepit old sofas under the stars and we tried to teach him English. An enthusiastic student, his approach was less successful than emotive as he focused on trying to learn the words by pointing at things and then not being able to repeat the word for them.

"Sofa," said Gerry pointing to our seat. "Sofa!"

"Hoover?" queried Mohammed.

"No. Sofa! Sofa!" said Charlie.

"Softer. Yes. Many fine springs. Yes."

"No, no, no. Sofa! Sofa! Oh – sofa-king what," said Gerry, giving up.

We all laughed and with that parted as best mates for the night, while Mohammed lay down and immediately passed out on the sofa in question which was apparently his bed.

***

The next day dawned warm and bright and we set off into Tetouan with Mohammed and his friend Hussan as our guides to sort out local insurance and to get some local money.

Trustingly we offered to pay two of Mohammed's young cousins to watch and wash both vehicles – the Land Rover windows apparently with grease – while we explored the bazaar!

Jim immediately went native, eliciting the comment "how bazaar" from Ched, buying a long woollen habit-like brown robe with a hood, called a Jalaba, while Gerry stocked up the larder, before Mohammed and Hussan led us to the edge of the city by a complicated back route – presumably in order to gain credence for their role as guides. After payment of a kind (a packet of filterless cigarettes), which were not well received and greeted with scowls, they waved us goodbye and confidently sent us on the wrong road to Algeria.

We eventually found our way onto the right road by seeing where the sun was and drove up through the Atlas Mountains and over a pass, which was shrouded in fog so thick that we couldn't see more than the length of the vehicle ahead. Then we hit thick snow, which was quite unexpected – by me at least. Weirdly, even in the most desolate areas shadowy figures, monk-like in their jalabas, loomed out of the gloom offering us bags of hashish which were probably the cause of the demise of two buses we passed embedded in roadside snowdrifts.

Back down the other side and into the more expected warm African climate that evening, we camped in a field and met a local chap who was most insistent in showing us where the 14th century road was. Perhaps if I had paid more attention in history at school it would have had some significance to me, but sadly it resembled the earth around and either side of it.

"Is here," he announced proudly, displaying his open palms towards the ground and beaming from ear to ear.

The scenery the next day was noteworthy though and bordered on the spectacular with abrupt and jagged mountainous terrain, cliff-edge roads and coral pink soil on the hillsides. Charlie and Ched took on the film crew's role and got many tracking shots, making full use of an essential fire engine modification that John Dennis had made back in Guildford – a sunroof. It provided a perfect platform for backward facing shots (and of course sun bathing for the more adventurous).

We arrived at Oujda and camped in a field near the Algerian border with the local children appearing from out of nowhere and performing outflanking manoeuvres around us to see what we were up to.

Supper preparations were well under way before Wink noticed that the water smelt of diesel – so not only was my cooking shit, it was incompetent too. This was rather a worrying development for everyone as Charlie patiently explained to me again which jerry cans were for diesel and which were for water. Being as I was in charge of supplies, this filled everyone with little confidence, but all was sorted out in the end and we settled down for a very uncomfortable night as the soil was very stony and even when we had cleared pebbles from the ground, they still appeared to be there. I noted in my diary that I was obviously not as hardened a traveller as I had thought.

***

The next morning we were through the Moroccan side of the border within one hour and no hassle, so perhaps we were professional travellers after all. The Algerians were also being very friendly and co-operative until their big cheese asked where the papers were to allow the fire engine into Algeria – it being too big to be classified as a car.

Oh dear, back to rookie status again with a bump.

Charlie, Jim, Wink and the Land Rover paperwork were all cleared and set off to Tlencen, in Algeria, to sort out the situation, while Gerry, Ched, Jamie and I remained in no-man's land playing card games, Ludo, reading and generally taking our cue from the border guards who were masters in practicing the noble art of inactivity.

On the return of the three musketeers, the customs men sped into action with all the enthusiasm of a sloth for the 100 meter dash and suddenly, we were cleared and into Algeria – a mere 12 hours after departing Morocco. We left the flying squad to sort out three Scotsmen who had arrived in a Land Rover *en route* for Tamanrasset with, judging by their total lack of kit, the sole objective of getting very, very drunk for Christmas.

That night, camping between Mohgnia and Tlencen, Wink tried a more overt form of team poisoning by making the tea with pure diesel.

"For God's sake, what a bloody shambles Jules," said Jim, ruefully staring at his poisoned cup of tea, but again we survived and lived to sleep through an uneventful night.

* * *

"Now this is more like it," I thought, much more like my imagined Africa as we headed for Tlencen, through Sardou and lunched in the desert. The road stretched away as far as the eye could see, marked only by the two lines of telegraph poles – like that scene in Alfred Hitchcock's film North by North West, except the golden fields of crops had been replaced by more sand than I could imagine.

Whether it was the sun or some hangover from his abscess, I do not know, but Gerry gave a roadside video interview to Ched about the wonders of Brighton nudist beach and then promptly took his clothes off and ran away to join the sand dunes in the distance.

The sand, I gather, was rather less user-friendly than that the pebble beaches of Brighton and Gerry soon returned and we set off with Ched driving for her first time at the wheel of the fire engine since Europe and we saw our first herd of camels and, somewhat bizarrely, and herd of black and white Fresian cows. We broke for camp in the desert (where else?) about one hundred kilometres from a place called Bechar and Ched and Wink imagined themselves striding across a Martian landscape as they returned with the only tree in several square miles for our fire.

That night we had the first of our dehydrated meals – a reasonable curry – although it went to my head as I then reversed the fire engine to shelter the camp from the wind, which had changed direction, but forgot to open the window before I looked behind me. "Nice bruise" was the only comment made by anyone, but they all seemed to say it rather a lot.

We now began to see why Charlie and Gerry used the phrase *that's Africa babe* the whole time, as we were learning that there is no reason to get stressed on the road. No-one, but no-one is in a hurry and bureaucracy rules, no matter how laboured its implementation might be.

We went through two very thorough checkpoints within the first hour as we neared Bechar – it being predominantly a military base and situated only 50 kilometres from Morocco – but still managed to arrive in time to meet the film crew at the airport, only to discover that they weren't there. They were fog-bound back in Heathrow.

We decided to get a few supplies and then head out of town to camp and wait for the crew's arrival. While shopping we met some British contractors from a company called Baxter Fell International, who were working on a project to build various police stations and prisons throughout Algeria. They hospitably invited us to their encampment where we showered and ate a great meal – much safer than doing it ourselves after the two recent 'diesel surprise' dishes I noted in my diary.

Refreshed, we drove out of town and camped in the desert some 20 kilometres to the south to await the arrival of the film team. However, having already experienced Baxter Fell's hospitality, we decided to leave Jim and Charlie guarding the fire engine and Land

Rover while we went back to the contractor's bar to get some of the Sahara dust out of our throats! There, we lost at bingo, lost Wink and Ched in a mêlée of various good-natured Geordies – one of whom seemed obsessed with suspenders and miniskirts and couldn't seem to understand why Wink wasn't wearing them – and then we lost ourselves in some form of local wine.

Not very brightly we managed to get stopped for speeding (or maybe being the only car going anywhere at all at that time of night) on the way back into the desert as we left town. Ched handled the situation perfectly with me lending some French and Gerry, not to be outdone, yelling from the back of the Land Rover "for Christ's sake don't let me breathe on him [the policeman]." We escaped without a fine and returned to the serenity of our desert camp.

CHAPTER 4

Tragedy & disaster – the Sahara proper

The first day of December was what my mother calls a "make do and mend day" as we waited in camp for the film crew who were now being held up by a more intractable issue than fog – airport bureaucracy in Algiers.

Our clothes were draped over bushes and rocks to dry, lockers were emptied of sand and cleaned out, which we were to discover is rather like trying to drain a pond using a sieve, and we chilled out over furious games of liar dice and took in the scenery. The desert here was rather less like the endless sand in David Lean's film, *Lawrence of Arabia*, and more like that which you see in the old cowboy westerns, with a few scraggly twigs/ bushes, and outcroppings of rock. But you could still see for miles and the feeling of being away from everything was quite palpable.

Jamie, who was by now fast growing into his cheery role as the expedition's grease monkey and showing considerable more ability for his role than the supplies wise guy, helped Charlie changed the oil on the fire engine and Land Rover, which was drained into a pit we had dug in the sand. That evening we lit a fire in the pool using a few sticks as wicks for a superb and safe night warmer.

But disaster struck.

Ched and Wink returned from a wood finding expedition across the rocks and somehow Ched tripped over and fell backwards into the fire. Being in a hole, her bum acting as a sort of plunger and the burning oil splashed up and out, covering her legs, arm and back.

The trip log and my own diary are both short on words describing the tragedy, but my memory is of things happening in an urgent, yet quiet manner. Ched was in shock and Gerry took control being the nearest to hand, checking the right course of action in our medical bible *Medicine: For Mountaineering & Other Wilderness Activities* and everyone taking orders as directed.

We urgently needed to get the hot oil off her body otherwise it would cool from the outside, sealing in the heat and intensify the burning to deeper layers of her flesh, causing even more damage than we could see at that moment. Working calmly but urgently, we had to peel off the oil covered skin – which having come away from her legs looked like thick stockings which had fallen down – while trying to keep sand of her exposed, raw flesh.

The images are something I will remember for ever and my overriding sensation was feeling rather scared following the accident, when we had time to think about things afterwards. It demonstrated the seriousness of our position, our vulnerability and it reminded me that, apart from the two professionals, we were basically naive amateurs out in the wild.

I noted in my diary that I was very reassured to have had Charlie and Gerry leading things and also that we had all done St John's Ambulance first aid courses to a high level of proficiency back in London before setting off. The expedition log entry merely reads:

Ched fell backwards into the fire and her legs and back caught light. Everyone surprisingly calm and responding to orders from Gerry, who seemed to take charge as we poured water on her and as we cut her burned clothes and skin away. Charlie, Gerry and Jim drove her to Baxter Fell and thence to hospital where Steve (Baxter Fell's medic) oversaw the treatment they gave her. Jamie, Wink and I remained at the camp awaiting news. Ched was stable and in good hands but suffering first degree burns on her legs, back and bum. Gave Charlie the SOS red cards for emergency contact numbers and settled down for an uneasy night.

Having been an insurance broker for almost five years prior to joining the expedition, I guess I had never really had first-hand experience of the value of insurance in the field, except for the odd holiday claim, and this was a rather rude introduction to the real world.

Some months before, one of my final jobs had been to draw up and place the team's insurance cover with an underwriter I knew at CIGNA – one of the world's leading insurance companies. They had generously agreed to take on the cover as a form of a sponsorship for nil premium, although they may have regretted this decision when all the final claims from the trip were in. It was without doubt the most essential piece of equipment we had and, perversely it seems in the light of the injuries and losses we sustained, we were incredibly lucky to have it.

***

It was an uneasy night, as I wrote in the log, with sleep very hard to come by and the morning dawned appropriately grey, but the mood in camp was lifted with the arrival of Graham, John and Tim (our film crew) and better news regarding Ched.

Charlie stayed in Bechar to call England and sort out a medical flight home for Ched – not as easy as imagined, bearing in mind this was a military zone and the air ambulance jet would need to land at the secure runway. The situation was greatly aided by the fact that Ched's father was a Government Minister back in the UK at the time. In the event, and with diplomatic incidents having been avoided, Charlie returned later that afternoon saying that Ched would be leaving for an English hospital by SOS Lear Jet in the morning.

The day in camp had been slightly odd. Intense winds and sand were blowing everywhere while everyone hunkered down in the Fire Engine cab, and avidly read English newspapers and mail from home, which the guys had brought out from England, while waiting for Jim and Charlie to return and trying not to think about the accident. Jim came back before Charlie at around teatime with two rather sour-faced policemen, to whom I explained in my halting French what had happened.

Anyone who has had the misfortune to be with me when I happily say that I can get by in a language will realise that I am more enthusiastic than linguistic. However, I am very pleased to say that where my schooling in history may have failed, French had won, as they seemed to understand what I was saying. Jim and I then followed the policemen to Kenedsa to file an official report in the police station.

Embarrassingly for them though, they promptly got us all lost travelling in a wide circle before joining the main road – which had been just over the rise all the time. They did not strike either of us as the most useful of policemen, so perhaps it was not surprising that they immediately decided to stop on the tarmac and write down out the train of events "to make easier your explanation at the station on paper," one of them haltingly explained in English.

The official reporting session basically meant Jim waiting outside whilst I spent two and a half hours in one of the two Kenedsa *gendarmerie* cells talking away in semi-fluent, but more probably effluent, French. Eventually we sorted out a statement which, without any change of expression throughout proceedings from the three policemen present, they seemed to accept so I read and signed the paper and they re-holstered their guns and stood up, beckoning me to lead them somewhere.

As this was a Muslim country, the basic thrust of their enquiries was to determine that we had not been abusing alcohol before the accident. Thankfully we had not and I assured them that we were a serious expedition and that the chief should come back to inspect the camp, check everyone's details and see our responsible approach for himself. One of my many faults is trying to be overly helpful and this was another example when a quick exit from the station – which is where the policemen were ushering me – would have been a better course of action.

We arrived at the campsite with the police chief in tow only to find Gerry and Tim absolutely smashed and Wink tending to Jamie who, having also resorted to some medicinal spirits, was wandering around bemoaning the loss of the tip of his thumb (which he had thoughtfully donated to the cabbage whilst preparing it earlier).

"Hi Jules – guess what?" was his greeting. "I've only bloody chopped the top off my thumb, haven't I?"

There then followed a rather amateurish French farce (without the sex) as Jim kept them all away from the policemen, steering them forcibly the other way around the fire engine as I showed the chief around the campsite and vehicles.

As it turned out, the new Land Rover proved to be the main point of interest and, after much chat with Jim (who seemed better at French than me) about what it was like to drive, comfort and capability, they soon went on their way.

The next morning Graham (plus his camera) went off with Jim and Charlie to see Ched onto the flying ambulance jet and we were left to break camp and meet them at Baxter Fell. Our situation was made more complicated by the fact that once they were out of site we discovered that the fire engine's battery was completely flat.

Jump starting a car is one thing, especially when you may even have a hill, but several tons of heavy goods vehicle is another matter altogether and although we did manage to push it backwards up a small incline, this was not enough.

There we were – alone in the desert, miles from anywhere, with a big, red fire engine which didn't work.

Imagine the surprise on the face of The Fly when he arrived in a truck to say his daily "hello." The Fly was a local so nicknamed because of the dense cloud which followed him around and who had visited us for three days to not altogether embracing welcomes from us.

We thanked him profusely for the jump start and made our rendezvous with the others at Bechar where once again we were showered and fed, before setting off to Taghit, a beautiful oasis town amongst the palm trees and even more like the Africa I had been expecting.

Ched's accident had strangely brought us closer together as a team and we were operating well. We prepared a fantastic meal from unnamed, assorted boil-in-the-bags whose wrappers had been destroyed by sand, so we played a game of Russian roulette – in the knowledge that one of them was a not very popular sweet and sour dish. We followed this by a round of the card game Old Maid, but with a more lavatorial name, which Charlie then lived up as he promptly got us well and truly stuck in the soft sand within minutes of breaking camp the next morning.

Two and a half hours later, after many attempts and losing the use of the fire engine's first gear in the process, we finally managed to cover the 150 yards back onto the road. It all proved good footage for Graham, although I am pleased to say that one shot of Gerry, Jamie & I mooning our displeasure of the morning's proceedings was destined for the editorially cutting room floor.

* * *

Getting stuck in sand or mud was one of our basic expectations and, as technical director, Warren Burton, had said on one of the expedition training weekends back in England, "Getting bogged down at some point is one of the only real certainties of a trip like this." As a result we carried four sand mats on the roof of the fire engine – these were three-by-one-metre sheets of corrugated iron, with two rows of four-inch holes down the length of them. These were to be placed under the wheels when we got stuck in sand or mud to gain traction and, hopefully, enable the vehicle to extricate itself under its own steam. An immense amount of digging was also required before placing the sand mats under the wheels, which could be repeated several times in succession as the vehicle inched forwards out of its mire.

On many occasions during the trip when using these mats, the vehicle would free itself and the mats would be spat out at random angles behind the wheels with a ferocity which could have easily chopped a leg in half, so the process was always potentially dangerous, as well as utterly exhausting.

In addition to the rudimentary mats, both the fire engine and Land Rover were fitted with electric winches at the front, for eventualities when sand mats alone would not do the trick. Both the winches and sand mats saw extensive use throughout Africa and proved to be invaluable tools.

* * *

We stopped for lunch just north of a town called Keizaz where, probably because he had spent so much time arsing around earlier, Jamie hadn't realised that the game of sand matting was over and got the fire engine stuck again. Was this the way we were to continue? Hopefully not, as Jim didn't see the funny side of it, nor did he like the fact that someone had christened the Land Rover Eric – a name that he had wiped from the dust on his bumper with much disdain.

That night we stopped in Timemoun at a special campsite, and had many beers in the hotel bar next door, having met up with the three Scottish guys from the border and got the good news on the hotel phone that Ched was safely back in England. She was being looked after in hospital and the story of her ordeal had made the national press back home. That night the mosquitoes also decided to party long and hard, on my forehead, which resembled that of a Klingon from Star Trek, the next morning. That too seemed to be 'Africa babe,' judging by the lack of sympathy I received over breakfast and Charlie's helpful travel tip:

"You're a bit of a tit for sleeping with you head under the Land Rover's bumper, Jules, as that's the sort of place mossies like to hang out."

I always seem to have been attractive to insects, especially mosquitoes and once, when on a canoeing trip down the Zambezi River many years later, I awoke to see the apex of my mosquito net black and swarming with them. Using it a bit like an icing bag I squeezed them all to death and it was only after red juices ran freely over my hand that I realised I must have been bitten and that it was my blood. My back resembled a severe measles infection and proved unbearably itchy for the next few days, but I am thankful that for me at least, the malaria precautions I was taking had worked – which was not something we could say on the fire engine trip further down on our odyssey through Africa.

***

By now the roads were beginning to deteriorate and driving was not helped by strong winds and drifting sand causing poor visibility, but it was exciting. Shelter for stopping was proving sparse and though we lunched in the lea of some gravel mounds, we still managed to get blown away while we enjoyed some real 'sand'wiches. Graham proved to be as keen a tea drinker as Jim and so now, whenever we stopped, he was on hand with a pot ready for *mashing* (one of Jim's favourite expressions and apparently the long brewing process without which tea will always be substandard).

Eventually the surface was so bad we were forced to drive off piste (the technical term for a desert route marked on a map – or on the ground by tyre tracks or huge black oil drums), which at least provided some spectacular film shots of the fire engine billowing clouds of dust and as it drove off into the sunset. We stopped to set up camp where there weren't too many tyre tracks and Charlie recounted a tale of two Germans whose tent was reversed over by a drunk driver in the night and so we slept as close to the vehicles as possible for protection.

We came down off the plateau we'd been driving on for the last couple of days to some breath-taking scenery and we drove around the base of an impressive 30 metre high Mesa stone pillar to great cinematic effect. Looking out of the window Jamie was heard to say "amazing, this is just like Arizona."

Towns and settlements in the desert are a welcoming sight – not so much because they have supplies, but because you then know where you are on the map – so we were pleased to reach Ain Salah for supplies, only to discover a minor hiccup – the whole place was closed for lunch. This oasis town had once been an important link in the trans-Saharan caravan route, but was now sadly past its prime. After some frantic bargaining with one of the few men we saw on the streets, we managed to persuade a local restaurant to sell us some bread and boiled eggs and some unnaturally bright, yellow lemonade so that we too could join in on the lunchtime break.

Despite being closed, there was lots going on and we met an Englishman who was hitching to Tammanrasset and a party of eight Danes who were doing a trip in Toyotas and trailers, one of which had surprisingly broken an axle as they reached 120kph off-piste.

South of the town we passed another fire engine (bloody cheek!) doing Sahara '87, but it wasn't nearly as impressive, nor was it British, so Wink drove on with her nose in the air. She later said that she hadn't even seen it, which wasn't much comfort for us passengers, but by then the sunroof had come into its own and for the last hour before camp we rode on top of the fire engine, where it was much cooler than inside the cab, but we couldn't talk above the noise.

We were on track for Tammanrasset, the centre of the Sahara, and the sand matting experience seemed to be behind us now, except for one soft patch, and we were only delayed in getting out as Jim had very public spiritedly offered to tow some locals out of a drift first. "But would we be able to have a beer on my birthday in two days' time?" I wondered selfishly.

***

Even by our standards we started early the next day, having breakfasted and broken camp by 6.30am and before the sun had had time to rise. The scene had been set for the day ahead as we became stuck for the first time. It was to prove a problematic day in the heat.

Inside the main storage area in the middle of the fire engine where the old water tank had been, and what was now the spare parts depot, nicknamed the sin bin for some unfathomable reason, the oil drum for the Land Rover gear box had become punctured. The leak was not spotted until half of the drum's contents had flooded the floor, which then gave way on one side and the liquid was decanted. This meant a re-pack of the entire contents to check if anything else was missing and to try to shore up the floor.

The fire engine then seized up totally with a blocked fuel pump and Charlie and Jamie leapt into action, mending both it and the back near side door's outer skin, which had detached itself from the door frame. The latter procedure provided new technical skills for us to learn as I saw a new use for an old item – gaffer tape.

John and Tim relinquished their filming duties and spent all that evening applying more gaffer tape to the rear door, whilst Charlie and Jamie spent the same time finding out what was causing the engine failures – three more had followed the initial seizure and we had been forced to camp at a gravel pit in a place called Arak. Having emptied the sin bin, fixed the floor and mended the punctured drum as best we could under Tim's guidance, he conspiratorially whispered: "Of course, you know what's wrong with the engine, don't you? Technically speaking, it's buggered."

Persistent setbacks are never good fun, but spirits remained high after cameraman Graham gave us his apparently famous (and certainly very good) imperson-ation of Peter Sellers' batman, Cato, in the original Pink Panther films and Gerry and Wink, whose knee, injured a few days earlier but now vastly improved, cooked up an impromptu feast.

**

The next day began with the relief that the fire engine was mended after Charlie, Jamie and Tim, who had left sound recording aside to assist, had been up most of the night nursing a broken fuel pump.

It was my birthday, so pressies were opened up on camera (another few shots destined for the cutting room floor), then everyone cleared up camp to the exciting audio taped story of *Masters of the Universe*, a children's adventure and birthday present from Ched and Wink. The tape retained its original characters but the accompanying book had been artfully updated by Wink to use the expedition team as the various characters.

However, it was to the more exciting sound of the fire engine's motor working well that we set off and, within half-an-hour, found a long stretch of actual tarmac. It was in fact so badly made that it appeared to have been accidentally spilled by the Algerians and it was with pure fluke that it resembled a road at all. One minor engine hiccup later, the fire engine was back on form and we had forgotten the less than flattering plaudits given to it the day before.

For the second time in the Sahara, we met up with Tamu, a Japanese biker travelling from Paris to as far south as he could go, and had sandwiches with him, before we discovered that the bottom shelf behind the FIRE sign at the back of the fire engine had given way. Having retraced our tracks and recovered the various items which the shelf had decided not to carry anymore, we spent a glorious afternoon filming with the camels roaming wild (they were actually bloody livid after Charlie had tried to drive between them "for artistic reasons") and we arrived at Tammanrasset, the centre of the Sahara, amazingly on schedule.

After eating we, set off in high hopes to the hotel for a beer which threw them into pandemonium as the bar had closed and the porter proved to be extremely unhelpful – *pas possible* being his response to all questions regarding beers. Luckily we were invited to have an evening drink with an overland travel group leader going the same way as us, so my birthday was not as dry as the surrounding countryside.

The next day was a rest day in Tammanrasset so most of us spent time in and around the markets in town. Gerry and I tried to rip off the man we thought to be the stupidest stall owner in history, but discovered his friends to be more savvy than us and not having any of it. I managed to haggle for a sword, cutting the chap down to 600 from 500 – perhaps confirming that it was I and not the stall holder who was actually the stupidest market trader in history.

Wink meanwhile made a headband out of sticky tape for a little kid, who professed he was her boyfriend for life, and then rescued from my sword fiasco by offering to swap her watch for two swords.

We thought that Charlie and Jamie had spent the day working on their tans as they were considerably darker than the locals when we returned, however, they had in fact spent all day cleaning, greasing and oiling the fire engine and were not overly interested in our tales of mysterious market traders.

At least we were prepared to subject ourselves to the vagaries of a film crew and the next morning we were awakened early by Fazah, the film crew's driver for the day. He was excellent at negotiating smooth rides for his team but not a great conversationalist and we debated his choice of music as being of little commercial interest outside his car. Chad Mig, a local group whose work seemed to consist of twanging some form of taut gut, which was probably still part of a live animal, only had the one song, but several different variations on the theme.

I had never really assessed the technical nature of filming before, but having spent six hours driving over and around the camera, seen the camera being tied to a pole for action wheel shots, I began to appreciate the length of time necessary for some of those TV wildlife films where the stars were not as compliant as we were.

We took one break and had an excellent session of sand skiing down a picture book sand dune and Gerry had a ball skiing behind the fire engine on sand mats before bidding a fond farewell to the film crew and giving them a huge shopping list to bring out with them next time they came to join us.

The short spells with us were probably the hardest art for the film crew. Documentary film making being what it is, we were almost certain to experience excitement, drama and danger when they weren't with us, but unfortunately the budget didn't allow for them to accompany us all the way so they had to make do with parachuting in for specific sections of our journey, while we were entrusted to a camera in their absence.

Predictably, as soon as we had parted, the fire engine packed up – the fuel pump, again. This time Charlie found the real cause of the problems – the tank switchovers, which allowed us to transfer fuel flow from one of the huge extra tanks to the other, was allowing air into the system. Air is not good for diesel units, which are sealed compression affairs, unlike petrol engines, which require air to function.

More gaffer tape later and, whilst camped between two large sand hills, we hit the first major supply problem of the trip – no more loo paper. As his was the most urgent need, Jamie was quickly on hand with some old newspaper which Charlie insisted on vetting first to make sure that there was nothing about cars or yachts on it. To Jamie's immense relief, there wasn't, and a potential crisis was averted.

CHAPTER 5

Getting stuck – car smuggling – an open air disco

During one of the many Saharan sand traps when we were really practising our sand matting and bucket and spade prowess, Jim, for some reason, decided to look under the bonnet of the Land Rover – possibly as a form of visual excuse as the overland travel group from Tammanrasset whizzed past us around mid-morning. Without reappearing from the engine, the Land Rover spoke to us, and considering it was the first time a car had spoken to anyone in the Sahara, its choice of language was alarmingly blue.

Jim had discovered a major setback, in that the Land Rover documentation appeared to register the vehicle with the wrong chassis number. This was especially disconcerting for us as the border guards at Niger were obsessively vigilant where car smuggling was concerned, and although we were legitimate, this was the type of error that often undid smugglers.

We paused mid-sand mat and cast various aspersions of guilt around into the blue Saharan air and then took the only course of action realistically available to us – to proceed to the border and take our chances. I noted in my diary that "having buried that hatchet we then spent the rest of the day burying the fire engine and Eric." We had all, Jim included, by now affectionately accepted the re-christening of the Land Rover.

As we approached the end of the day, completely exhausted from the unrelenting exercise, we showed willing by helping two Swedes in a Nissan, who were over their axles in soft sand, and then promptly got ourselves stuck, just for old times' sake. Having averaged around 15 miles per hour that day, we pitched camp near a group of nine French travellers (whose Land Rover weighed six tonnes) and Jim spent most of the evening memorising the chassis number on the documents for a 'reading' from underneath the engine, once we were at the border.

***

We sneakily decided to throw the previous evening's camaraderie out of the window and to make an early start for a change to steal a march on the Frenchies. Charlie took the fire engine over a small ski jump, which to be fair to him was camouflaged by the flat dawn light, and we shattered one oil jerry can and split the big water one. Not to be outdone, the fuel pump then started to leak again and the sand resumed its ability to suck in heavy objects, and so it was that we haltingly reached the border point at In-Guezzam, which had by then closed for lunch.

Amazingly we passed through the Algerian side of the border, with Jim slightly more relieved than everyone else and we reached Assamaka at about teatime. Our hopes were raised as we cleared customs within half an hour, only for them to be dashed by the closure of the passport office with ours the very next documents to be stamped.

As we sat contemplating life and watching trucks and cars approach the passport office from 360 degrees – despite all of them having set off from Tammanrasset, the same direction as us – we consoled ourselves with cold beers from an impromptu café in the sand. Some newly made Swedish friends invited us to join in a communal camp that consisted of the four of them, two Germans and some other French guys.

The party spirit was heightened when one of the Germans was told to stop blowing his trumpet about how expert he was in desert conditions and a French hunter showed great maturity at some minor jest about shooting finches in Paris, by standing up in a huff, tipping his beer on the ground and stomping off with his camp lights and leaving us in silent darkness for about two seconds before everyone burst out laughing.

He condescended to re-join us for the meal that Gerry and I had cooked for 14, despite having already eaten and not providing any of the ingredients. However, he did set up some arc lights so we were blinded throughout dinner and whilst team camaraderie was forged Jim was amused to be taught how to make tea 'properly' by two of the Germans.

***

Of the Europeans, we were the first through the border, with Jim both visibly and physically relieved not to have been incarcerated for car smuggling, and we set out for Arlit – a place only remarkable for its uranium mines. By the time we arrived at the end of the 1980s they were coming to the end of their profitability, so we were not expecting a huge amount from the place. But we were wrong.

Driving through African villages and townships is an extraordinary experience, with dogs, chickens and children dashing this way and that and all apparently keen to be the first to get squashed under the wheels. Happily, this game was never won by anyone during the expedition, but we were besieged by a swarm of children as we approached Arlit. All were yelling *"Un cadeau! Un cadeau!"* and leaping dangerously up at the fire engine windows – another good point about the vehicle choice, these being a good two metres off the ground and so inaccessible to all but the most determined of hands.

Having persuaded them that we weren't Santa Claus and left them in as high spirits as before we arrived – despite the lack of *cadeaux* – we went off in search of a beer and met up with another overland team who showed us the campsite and promised to take us to the nightspot in Arlit. Probably in anticipation of a great evening out, Wink and I hurriedly cooked probably the worst meal of the trip so far and left Jim to wash up while we, with Gerry, went off to paint the town any colour at all at *Le Cheval Blanc*, the local nightspot.

More interesting than the uranium mines, *Le Cheval Blanc* was the place in town for absolutely everything – except presumably precious ore itself – and we danced in the enclosed open-air square in between a band playing at one end and a bar opposite. Though better than Chad Mig, the band's musical approach was hugely original with their singer punctuating verses by being alternately sick to one side of the stage and doing dope deals the other.

The people of Arlit though were very friendly and the evening was a great success, although if we never see that particular overland travel group team again in a bar, it may well be too soon for some!

The next morning Gerry wasn't feeling well at all, probably due to the food at the white horse, and the Land Rover decided to join in the events by developing an air leak of its own. This was more easily sorted out than Gerry's stomach and we made good progress to Agadez, where we stopped for refreshments and some surreptitious photos of its famous raven-covered mosque (taking photos of which was highly illegal and most disrespectful). Most buildings of religious significance are closely protected from cheap tourist photography, but it still makes me laugh today, when I try to take illicit photos, at how melodramatic and obviously unnatural I am at secret agent stuff. This is a point which would have been lost on the Zimbabwean colonel who later in the trip was to arrest us all and impound the fire engine for spying.

By now the roadside checkpoints were becoming more common and our passports were getting well-inked but it was increasingly worth it as we camped out in the wilds near a four foot termite mound, cooked off an open fire, ate Charlie's pancakes for pudding and spent the evening watching shooting stars from the warmth of our sleeping bags. I am always surprised at how cold it gets at night in the desert, but our sleeping bags were superb.

* * *

Not to be outdone by the Land Rover's small technical hitch, the fire engine failed fairly proficiently the next day and eventually, after much patient tinkering and use of the now all too familiar technical vernacular, Charlie determined that the leak was actually somewhere between the main tank and the fuel pump. At least he seemed relieved to have found the cause of our stuttering progress, and the mood rubbed off on us as we bizarrely cheered a huge flock of vultures feeding off a dead camel by the side of the road and photographed our first true Tuareg. Again rather obviously, as he was hitching his camel to a post before having a drink.

As we passed through some very small villages with great names like Ahole and Dodon Doutche, the countryside gave way to a fairly green scene, with crops growing plentifully and a particularly mature word game inside the vehicles:

"Amaizing."

"Wheat till you see the next field."

"That's barley a joke."

"Oat to be anywhere but here."

"That's corny."

Travelling by road was a great relief and after a day of around 500 kilometres, we arrived at Niamey, the capital city of Niger, and camped with a very sombre warning from the night watchman, who warned us about a "Tiefman. Him no black man. Him tiefman."

Luckily for us, tiefman did not trifle with strange travellers in a big red fire engine.

CHAPTER 6

Marketing heaven – an outbreak of war – Christmas in style

Niamey was a pleasing place to hang out, as it turned out we had to whilst Charlie sorted out our EAS supply drop in Kano. We left our passports at the French Embassy for Central African Republic (CAR) visa stamps and were therefore limited in where we could go and we could do, so we split up, with some staying and swimming in the Grand Hotel's pool, and the rest of us off to trawl the markets for interesting trinkets.

Interesting trinkets, however, were in short supply – probably because the market we chose was more of the fruit and vegetable type, with a small area for personal hygiene, but at least this provided us with some superb names for local fragrances. Great packaging and superlative imagery accompanied such unheralded perfume brands as *Shag, My Only Man, Grotto and Sex Appeal*.

The textile market on the other hand was a bit like an explosion in a paint factory, with every conceivable pattern and colour used, but the gilt was slightly taken off the gingerbread when closer inspection revealed that almost all of the local fabrics on display had been screen printed in England.

That evening we spent the night chatting with a retired couple from Yorkshire who had decided that you were never too old for adventure and were travelling around the world and making our own efforts look a little cosseted and pampered.

***

Having secured and collected our CAR visas, we set off for Nigeria and the town of Kano, where, if flights had gone according to plan, EAS should have delivered a spare fuel pump and gear box for the fire engine, along with new carnets (official vehicle insurance and registration papers) and documentation for the Land Rover.

Despite merely having to follow our earlier route back from Niamey, our progress was casual and we camped just east of Dogon Doutche. Jim was a little edgy about returning here as he had made a mess of their checkpoint registration book when we had passed through before, but there were no problems and we picked for our campsite a dry wadi (the local name for a water hole). Charlie had great fun playing with the winch – he said it was to check Tim's mending of it after Bechar (at the mention of which Jamie just scowled) – but he was just messing about with it and using the line to pull up small bushes and trees for firewood.

Jamie's scowl was to last until the next morning when he discovered that he had unwittingly picked the worst spot for sleeping – right on an ants' nest, although he himself escaped being bitten and had slept well.

Having broken camp early, "to beat the border rush" as Wink put it, the Land Rover immediately appeared to have got lost. After casting good natured aspersions about having navigators who were more used to being on boats than roads, Jim and the Land Rover appeared having been checking that we had left the campsite clean.

We made the Nigerian border at Maradi without further incident and what a relief it was to be back with English speaking officials – or was it? After a tense half an hour spent in customs due to that damned registration document of the Land Rover's and Jim's dramatic rendition of 'reading' the numbers from under the engine, we are cleared again and smuggled the Land Rover inside Nigeria, only to be stopped at a checkpoint a mile or so down the track with the fire engine's carnet not in order. The border guards had forgotten to sign it, so Charlie and Jim hastened back to make it legitimate.

We camped just off the road in some scrubland where Charlie, Gerry and Jamie decided to have the sweet and sour boil-in-the-bags for supper. I noted that they were mad fools and felt suitably rewarded later as this particular *oeuvre* proved to be Charlie's undoing. I solemnly recorded in the expedition log that he saw the light after that and has joined the ever-growing band of those team members disenchanted with this particular form of Epicurean disaster.

* * *

The next morning we had a novel reason for making an early and somewhat hasty start – we were woken by the sound of sporadic gunfire just over the ridge from our campsite. Gerry became the conflict reporter on the front for the benefit of our own video and explained that war had broken out over the odour from my shoes, which had mistakenly been taken as a sign that a chemical attack was in progress. The offending shoes had been discovered the day before when the unlucky wearer had received a one inch thorn through the sole of one and resorted to taking them off for sympathy. None had been forthcoming and it was only due to some particularly fast talking on my part that the party had continued with all six members and my shoes.

Having shoved our kit into the fire engine, none the wiser for the real reason for gunfire, Gerry finished off his war report with an athletic roll down the hill and leap into the passenger seat, we made an unnoticed getaway from the presumed army manoeuvres and arrived in Kano without incident.

We were led to the campsite in Kano there by a chap on a Wall's Ice Cream bicycle, whom Jamie nearly ran over whilst waving to some of the overland crowd from Tammanrasset, who, along with another group and an Australian motorbiking couple we knew, were already camped there.

Rich, the Australian bloke, seemed to have recovered well from our first meeting in the Sahara, where we had given him some antibiotics to reduce the swelling caused by a bug which had become wedged up his nose whilst riding at speed. His eye was still bloodshot, but we appeared to have been reasonably proficient in our medical attention and the swelling was gone – as, we could only presume, was the bug itself. It was yet another reminder of the type of ridiculous danger people that faced on the road.

The next day, Charlie and Jim went to the airport to see if our Red Cross parcel had arrived. As well as essentials like chocolate and books, we were also waiting for a new gear box and fuel pump for the fire engine and some contact lenses for Charlie. It was unfortunately an abortive trip and they returned empty-handed to find Jamie up to his elbows in grease under the fire engine and Gerry making burgers from the savoury mince and some local bits he had found. I was wandering around the campsite looking in vain for sympathy over the state of my forehead – which had swollen to gargoyle proportions having again been bitten to the other side of hell by mosquitoes, after I had fallen asleep with my head once more under the overhang of a vehicle – this time the fire engine.

So far on the trip, we had not had much luck with meeting packages at airports – first in Germany and now here in Nigeria, and it was only by perseverance on our third visit to Kano International Airport, that we discovered the goods had in fact arrived at customs and were due to be cleared on 22nd December, fingers crossed.

But – to put things in perspective, back in England, Ched was due her first skin graft operation and we were awaiting news from that with both our fingers and toes crossed.

While passing the time in between airport visits, Wink and I proved still to be a little on the amateur side when it came to shopping as we tried to use up some of the local currency. We spent about 15 minutes trying on hats from a local roadside stall to the increasingly hysterical amusement of the locals. Not dissuaded from our intentions to enhance our wardrobes, it was only upon deciding upon two colourful items that we discovered they were laughing at us, not with us. The stall, it turned out, was the local hat laundry and almost every item that we had tried on, was in fact waiting to be picked up to be cleaned.

Captain Wada, the EAS pilot who flew in our Red Cross parcel, couldn't stay, but lived up to Gerry's nickname for him "Wada Good Bloke" by saying that we could have a meal on him that night. As he wasn't actually there we had it on a table in the Central Hotel instead and experienced some great service, being the first in and the last out.

Following my experience the previous night we decided it was mosquito-nets for all from now on.

* * *

In anticipation of leaving Kano the next morning, Wink and I went to the fruit market to stock up on fresh items and had a curious introduction to religion as our taxi driver played a song whose main chorus was: *How do you treat your God? - Like a G.O.D. or a D.O.G?* To say he sang along doesn't really do justice to singing, but he was certainly full of praise for his 'sweet Jesus', as he delivered us unscathed through the traffic mayhem and a strange backstreet rout at the Kurmi Market – which had apparently been operating on the same site for several hundred years.

The market proved to be a more fruitful ground for worship for us as, although you could buy almost anything you wanted there, we were delighted by a specific stall which was showcasing more exotic perfume products including our old favourite, *Shag*. The stall also had some new ones including something in a long black tube called *Stud*, a soap powder featuring a local woman with no arms, curiously named *Venus de Milo* and some biscuits called *Finger Me*.

Meanwhile back at the airport, Charlie and Jim had picked up the crate of spares and box of goodies, and had a less amusing morning clearing customs – only to be exacerbated back at the fire engine by the discovery that Charlie's contact lenses, and some chocolates, were missing from the box.

Despite this setback we were ready, so we bid farewell to Kano. Shades of Paris floated back to us as we drove out of the city as Jim steered us through a labyrinth of roads – left a bit, right a bit, etc. – all of which seemed exactly the same.

Much later, we eventually moved passed the final dwellings and turned off road to camp in a huge sand pit, nearly running over a local who leapt into the spotlight, started gesticulating wildly and jabbering and shouting loudly at us. Whilst not fluent in his language, but more proficient in some globally recognised sign language of our own, he grudgingly stepped aside and we made camp.

By this stage, the Land Rover was very low on fuel and after several attempts to fill up in the fantastically named villages of Combe, Bin and Mudi, along the way to the border, we used the last of the fuel jerry cans from the fire engine. At Mudi, the last of these villages, we stopped to buy some fresh meat and Jamie and I surreally helped some chap fill in his football pools coupon outside the meat shack, while Wink was besieged by a hoard of children.

Just outside the town, the tarmac stopped and the road became a very rocky dirt track for the last 15 kilometres to the border, where the Nigerian police were friendly. The customs official was completely off his rocker on something and, while we had no problems having our paperwork approved by him – to great big grins and laughter – we played an interesting game guessing where he was going to place his stamp down and moving our passports to that area of the desk.

The Cameroon side at Bakoula could not have provided more of a contrast, with each one of the soldiers looking at everything at least twice. While this was going on, some scruffy bloke appeared from behind the hut and started jabbering on at the window about a carnet. Slightly alarmed by his closeness I felt resolutely proud of my defence and I steadfastly refused to give it to him until Gerry pointed out that it was actually I who was in the wrong.

"You dozy bastard," he said, somewhat surprisingly to me and not the beggar beyond the windscreen. "Jules – he is the customs man."

After this clarification we smoothed through the border post in a mere three hours and drove in darkness down what appeared to be dried rapids and a waterfall, and I remember wondering if this was the shape of things to come? We camped by the side of a reservoir, just before we could see the tarmac road begin again, and ate our fresh chicken.

* * *

Christmas Eve dawned and with the sun came the keeper of the reservoir who in confident terms told us that we were forbidden to camp there. "Dangerous. Dangerous. And just not right," he told us.

"It's alright mate," explained Charlie. "We aren't camping here now – we are leaving."

This seemed to placate him and before long we were back on a beautifully smooth tarmac road. However, just over the dam and around a bend, having travelled for about one kilometre, the tarmac ended and it was then a bumpy slog along 15 kilometres of dirt road and through various small settlements, with Wink shouting *"Joyeux Noel"* out of the window and waving to all the locals.

Despite this oral handicap, many waved back and we arrived safely at Garona with four minutes to spare before the banks closed at noon, and we completed a mad scramble to change some money.

With complete disregard for Christmas spirit, Gerry was then mugged whilst buying bread in the market place, and there followed a hectic chase in and out of market stalls, with people scuttling in all directions until a helpful local managed to stick out his basketful of vegetables and up-end Gerry's assailant. The money was returned and Charlie and Jim and Gerry went off to the police station – with the now hobbling and deflated would-be criminal, to sort out the paperwork. Their impression from the look of the police hospitality towards the mugger, was that he would not be walking for a some time to come.

Having planned our Christmas break way in advance, we miraculously arrived at the selected game park before Christmas Day and drove to our home for the festive season, *Le Buffle Noir Hotel.* In celebration, Gerry cooked creatively carved chips and we retired to the hotel bar where wine, dancing and parlour were the order of play, before retiring to the campsite to collapse in some dishevelment and await the arrival Father Christmas and his sleigh.

Parlour games had become one of the main evening entertainments for us and we were all comfortable in each other's company by now, so even the most ridiculous ones were keenly contested. Ibble Dibble, a memory game whose forfeit was marking you face with either a burnt cork or shaving foam, was a firm favourite by now, as were Ludo and liar dice – which despite being less messy, were also both hysterically fought.

***

Christmas day, 1987, began slowly for the same reason that other Christmases the world over do, but we managed to get some semblance of order together (i.e. we put the kettle on to boil) after only a couple of hours.

Charlie's breath would have been better described by a Billy Connolly rant, but for simplicity's sake it could have been said to come straight from the Devil's bottom, and so we put him in charge of not talking to us and of finding the World Service on the fire engine's radio so that we could listen to the Queen's speech.

Despite being somewhat smaller in stature than the traditional Father Christmas image and with no beard, Gerry played Santa by getting presents out of one of the rafting bags in the fire engine's sin bin, while the rest of us washed the dried shaving foam and burnt black cork from our faces. Having been in the sin bin for some time, Gerry was found to be having a few difficulties in moving around, having apparently strained a hamstring from dancing the night before, but he soldiered on and soon we had a pile of brightly wrapped pressies all around us.

Anne Lewis, Jamie's mother, Alex da Silva and Luli Thompson had done us proud back in England. As a new cassette of Christmas carols rang out over the campsite from the fire engine's hi-fi, paper was ripped open and chocolate was guzzled to cries of delight and disdain as one package revealed a magazine of distinctly adult content about an inappropriately named woman called Tina Small. The boys were happy and Wink's plaintive cries of "Where's my naughty mag?" were ignored as we discovered that all six of us had been given a packet of condoms. We were speculating as to the thoughtful nature of their provision and on their potential use, when Gerry got it wrong trying to put one over his head and inflate it from his nose. He did achieve his objective though, which was to impersonate part of Tina Small's anatomy.

The French girls we had met in the bar the night before, came over and took us down to a spectacular waterfall and natural rock water slide on the river, where we swam, shaved and shampooed (a more hygienic version of Jim's daily 3 'S's mantra) for the rest of the day. Jamie accidentally delighted the girls with an unannounced introduction from the flies of his boxer shorts and then it was back to the camp for a general smarten up before our proper Christmas supper at the hotel.

In the restaurant, Gerry and Wink did their best to explain Ibble Dibble to the French families eating there, with reasonable clarity – but a total lack of comprehension, and then we ate a magnificent feast of roast guinea fowl. To say that the service was slow would have been a compliment, but we weren't going anywhere until noon the next day and crackers, streamers, silly hats, a few beers and a bottle of champagne from David Henriques saw us through, along with a public game of the now obligatory Ibble Dibble in which everyone at the camp took part.

CHAPTER 7

Major fire engine damage – New Year – roadside curiosities

Boxing Day provided us with the first puncture of the trip and all honours went to the Land Rover – before we had left the campsite. Jim soon had it fixed and Jamie, Gerry and I went for a final skinny dip in the river and we left the *Buffle Noir* on schedule at noon.

All afternoon we saw huge piles of cotton left drying by the side of the road, except for near the checkpoints, so we knew when we were approaching one, and at our second of the afternoon we met up with an Encounter Overland Land Rover coming north towards us. The driver, Mick Squire, and Charlie exchanged pleasantries and from his comments, we were pleased to have been in the comparative luxury of two vehicles as his team smile out from a game of sardines they were obviously playing in the back of his truck. He also had good news about the roads ahead in Zaire being not too bad, so things were looking bright and our plan to miss the rainy seasons, which made much of Central Africa almost impassable, was also looking good.

In celebration of the end of the tarmac road and the start of the corrugations, we stopped for lunch at a place called Nqundiri in a very pleasant garage forecourt - and to think I used to be rude about people in England having a cup of tea in the lay-by.

Corrugations are the most uncomfortable road surface on which we drove as they are caused by the wheels of a vehicle bumping up and displacing sand back and forth to form little valleys, or corrugations. As more wheels go over the section the originally stable pattern is spread out further and migrates with the travelling direction providing a very bumpy surface on which to drive and a huge desire from those going over it for smooth tarmac or concrete again.

Just before we pulled into another sandpit campsite that night, Charlie said he could smell my feet and a major panic ensued inside the fire engine; but, after a nervous check I was cleared and the source of the obnoxious smell was identified as coming from the cooking in the roadside villages. Sadly I was obviously going to be the first point of call for any smells for the rest of the trip, but at least for the moment, I was innocent.

We were under a certain amount of time pressure now as our visas expired the next day, so tempers frayed a little when Jim and Wink took a wrong turn and disappeared just before the border post. They soon joined us from another angle altogether, perhaps having got inspiration from the approaches to checkpoints in the Sahara, and some polite but exceedingly officious CAR guards greeted us. One of them - a gigantic man mountain - took a shine to Wink, who after a plea for help was rescued by Jamie and we watched helplessly as the soldiers then took the vehicles apart. Another guard, who appeared to be mentally on vacation in another galaxy on another planet, kept insisting that he should have a torch, but he finally left us alone after a touch of Gerry's gentle persuasiveness: "Listen mate. Why don't you just bugger off?"

* * *

We left our latest sandpit campsite at the crack of dawn on good roads and we reached the 12 kilometres police checkpoint at Bangui early in the afternoon. This was by far the most organised checkpoint we had encountered in Africa so far, with all the right forms and everyone knowing what they were doing. We left our passports there for next day collection and set off to a campsite at Delango and finished pitching our tents some 15 minutes before the heavens opened with an absolute deluge of biblical proportions. Jim and Wink had luckily managed to use their meteorological knowledge and forewarn us of this natural water hazard. However, they seemed to be showing some signs of memory failure – or as Wink put it:

"Um....that's a cumulus something cloud. I remember it from my A-levels...um...and I think that means rain... you know, the green crosses?"

As it happened, we were destined to be almost marooned be in Delango for several days – but not by the rain. Our visas were not ready the next day, on top of which a cost of 2,500 Central African Francs (about US$5) each had appeared from nowhere, the Land Rover puncture repair was playing up and the fire engine was about to suffer serious damage.

At least the campsite was complete with creature comforts and the showers proved to be functional – albeit hazardous to the user as the water could be stopped whatever stage you were at by turning a tap in the basin next door. This plumbing anomaly proved a good game as the days went by.

On the first day we split into teams and got organised. Jim and I found a garage to finally mend the Land Rover's puncture once and for all, the cause of which turned out to be a huge nail, which we couldn't spot. Jamie and Charlie got mucky greasing and mending the gear box in the fire engine and Gerry and Wink went shopping and found the local supermarket to be ruinously expensive.

After supper we became the focal point of the campsite and numbers swelled around the table as Wifey and Mick, two drivers from commercial overland expeditions who were also staying in the campsite, and several members of the other groups migrated in for an impromptu party – luckily the only cheap provision there was beer.

Somehow the bonnet catch on the Land Rover had broken, so the first task the next morning was to fix it. While dealing with the problem we relocated to a higher point in the campsite and as we backed the fire engine into a space there was a huge, wrenching crack from underneath. Thinking that a front wheel drive shaft had gone, Jamie and I started unpacking the sin bin to get out a spare but, while locating the item, we heard a muffled cry from beneath out feet.

Charlie had discovered to his horror that it was in fact the prop shaft which had sheared off and we didn't have a spare. The prop, or drive shaft, is a long, metal rod about as thick as your leg which, in a vehicle like the fire engine where the clutch and gear box (or transmission) are mounted directly on the engine, connects to a final drive in the rear axle. The shaft rotates within a brace and without it you can't move. So Charlie's muffled cry, which was in fact more of a long, wailing journey through the lexicon of the world's great swear words, was wholly justified.

Jim and Charlie took the two halves (each piece now looking like small cannon's barrel) to the French garage where we had got the puncture mended. The proprietor shrugged and seemed hopeful of sorting something out the next day.

"I've seen much worse," he said confidently. And then, rather curiously: "I have no fear."

So there we were to stay and we resigned ourselves to seeing in the New Year at Bangui.

At least we could get the paperwork sorted out and be ready to go when it was mended, so Jim and I arrived at the designated hour of 11.30am to pick up the visas from the checkpoint.

"Fifteen minutes, my friend. All done."

So we sat down to wait, however, after about ten minutes, two Italians were told to come back after lunch and, following a brief enquiry, the man said he had meant to tell Jim the same and that he would also see us then. *That's Africa babe*.

On the dot of 3pm Jim, me and Fausto, one of the Italians who was driving overland to climb Mount Kilimanjaro, were back at the visa office with books to read in anticipation of further delay, but amazingly, the papers were ready. We returned in high spirits, only to find Charlie in bed and feeling very ill.

The next day Charlie's fever was worse, but the garage seemed to think the prop shaft would be ready that afternoon, so Gerry and Jim took Charlie off to see a doctor at the US Consulate while we waited. Being helpful souls they pointed out that the MD was only for US personnel so they went to the Pasteur Institute to get a blood test and luckily it proved negative for malaria, which was our chief concern.

Malaria is quite a common disease in Sub-Saharan Africa and is spread via the bite of a mosquito. Fever, hot and cold sweats, and headaches are the most common symptoms and, whilst we were all taking daily preventative medicine in the form of some disgusting-tasting tablets called Paludrine and Chloroquine, this was a luckier result than we would experience a bit later on in the trip.

With Charlie safely back in his sleeping bag, we returned to the garage and frustratingly found it closed, which meant that with the next day being New Year's Day and a public holiday, we would not see our prop shaft again for two days.

"Ah well," we chorused in unison. "That's Africa babe."

A friend of Wink's from back in Scotland had arrived in the campsite on another overland trip which was only meant to be passing through, but we persuaded them to stay and see in the New Year with us, rather than go for their pre-arranged campsite.

After supper it was straight to the bar for a few beers, which promptly ran out (as the barman was off to a party) so we gathered round the fire and celebrated with our collective supplies and saw in 1988 in with a selection of travellers' tales and fireside games.

In true schoolboy fashion, my favourite was by far the most juvenile. It involved sneaking off to stealthily remove some of the other campers' fly sheets from their tents and replacing them the wrong way around so that confusion reigned when the occupants tried to get into them after a few drinks.

The owners whose tents they were, proved to have an equally silly sense of humour and having entertained us with their confusion they joined us bringing a large beer supply.

Gerry and I snuck off to play one more joke, having decided to take one tent down altogether and move it somewhere else, but we were surprised to discover that the occupants had already started their New Year with a bang of their own.

Gerry and I made New Year resolutions to be more grown up in the coming year while Jim decided to give up smoking, which after some 26 years puffing away at ciggies and his pipe was the immediate start of a bet on how long he would last.

**

1988 dawned quietly, and from several perspectives in the team, rather biblically – in the beginning was light, followed by pain behind the eyes and then the general symptoms of a hangover. Gerry opened his speaking account for the year with a rather mumbled: "Whothe tongue ith thith in my mouth? - It doethn't theem to fit."

Once again thanking my lucky stars that I did not seem able to get headaches or hangovers, I popped the kettle quietly onto the cooker and the whispered "Tea, or Coffee?". Grunts and groans according to preference were received and translated and the overland team came over to inform us that they were off to the Red Cross mission in town where they had a "proper, civilised campsite" and we accepted their invitation to join them for supper to see its luxury for ourselves.

Charlie was feeling better, but tired, and everyone suffered from the lack of soft drinks at the bar – the barman thus proving that he had no idea of what was expected of him on a New Year's Day. That evening we arrived at the Red Cross mission at 7.30pm to find that they had eaten our meal and that only banana and pineapple crumble was left.

Hungrily back in our camp, we wound up the day chatting to a group of Germans, who were smoking some grass with another guy we had met on Boxing Day in Cameroon. He said that he had never tried dope before and then complained loudly to no one in particular, that it did nothing for him. Half an hour later he stood up looking slightly the worse for wear and we all watched him slowly and very deliberately navigate the long route back to his VW Kombi-van, a distance in reality of only about three metres and then, five minutes later, we heard an almighty crash as he fell out of bed and somehow opened the door and tumbled out of the van. 1988 had certainly begun with a vengeance for him.

* * *

We were up at first light and made ready for the off while Jim, and a much more-spritely Charlie, went to pick up the mended prop shaft from the French garage owner. He smilingly produced it in exactly the same state as it had been left with him, with the helpful additional diagnosis that it was broken. Not being with them I couldn't swear to this, but my guess was that they did not say "that's Africa babe."

Having gained some extra time for repacking, we did just that, making the fire engine ready for departure again and having great fun filling up all nine jerry cans with water and leaving several people stranded in the shower. Charlie and Jim dashed around town trying to find another garage, which they eventually did, and worked with the owner to help him cut down to size a prop shaft of similar width, which was then welded to the end of our existing shaft. This fairly Heath Robinson affair was then dutifully bolted into place by Jamie. (William Heath Robinson was an artist mainly remembered for his overly-complicated and unfeasible contraptions which were unlikely to ever work in reality.)

However, the prop shaft was not a good fit and we discovered that travelling at anything over 1700 rpm produced very un-Beach Boys-like vibrations. This uncomfortable percussion, coupled with the fact that the fire engine was still without first gear, meant for some slow travelling, with a top speed of around 35mph. Despite this, we managed to make good mileage and the end of the day found us camped amongst some six foot high, mushroom shaped termite mounds, within a day's drive of the border. Technically speaking termite mounds, rock hard and made from a mixture of earth, saliva and faeces, are overspills from underground nests, but they contain air tunnels which act as cooling chimneys for the whole next and incubation chambers beneath.

A local man disrupted our meal trying to sell us a roast tortoise, but soon disappeared when I explained: "We are not about to shell out on cooked meat when we are turtley full from have already eaten." A smattering of rain cleared the air, in much the same way that Charlie's post illness bowel movement cleared it of cicada chirruping and birdsong, and there was just time for a few hands of bridge before bed in preparation for an early morning start – just to make a change.

The tarmac finally ran out at the town of Sibut (pronounced see-boot) and, as we drove through the surrounding villages we began to see a curious selection of roadside offerings, which made the previous night's roast tortoise seem rather bland and conventional. There was a monkey strung up by its tail, several birds about which we did not like speculate, an animal which looked alarmingly like a large rat, something unidentifiable but roughly the size of a spaniel, a roasted pig and one would-be wild offering – a mongoose which hesitated between, playing lemming down the bank of the road, and chicken back into the grass.

We stopped for refreshments at one neat little village, which, despite having a disco floor and a huge, walk-in fridge, unfortunately had no electricity, so the Coke was rather warm but strangely good. The barman, when I asked if I could take the bottles out to the bar, asked in all sincerity, "pour quelques jours?" and was much relieved, though somewhat confused when they were returned a mere ten minutes later.

The closer we got to the border, the worse the road became, gradually descending into one long run of bone-jarring corrugations and we again thanked our lucky stars for the relative comfort of the sprung coach seats we John Dennis had installed in the fire engine back in Surrey.

Less rough dirt did present itself as we approached the exit border post for the Central African Republic – the city of Mobaye, on the Ubangi River, which is the largest tributary of the Congo River (or Zaire River as it was then known) – and so we pulled into the Catholic mission there in a relatively smooth manner. Unfortunately their response to our request to spend the night was one less smooth and relatively uncharitable word –"*Non.*"

So we stayed in the courtyard of the *auberge* down the road, where the owner insisted we play his cassette for him as loudly as we could on our stereo. Having no tape machine of his own he wasn't sure what was on it and so we were somewhat nervous as to the musical genre, but much to our surprise it turned out to a present from an earlier overland group and contained classics from Van Morrison, Journey and Gerry Rafferty, so we weren't too put out.

I noted in my dairy that Charlie was the first to formally crumble and had finally had enough of dehydrated/boil-in-the-bag meats so heavy flavour disguises would be needed in future, although why I wrote this is beyond my memory as my cooking was certainly the least rewarding night in the culinary rota.

CHAPTER 8

Zaire – well and truly bogged down – Kisengani

Owning to the proximity of the border/river crossing, it being only a few hundred meters from the *auberge*, we had the luxury of setting off at around 9am and, clearing customs with ease, we were soon loaded onto the roll-on-roll-off ferry. The captain was a bit difficult as he was not keen to accept French francs for the trip, but Jim smoothed the way with some calm reasoning (talking very deliberately, loudly and slowly) and we made it across without worry.

The Zaire policemen were also relaxed as Gerry popped back over the border to get some change while Charlie and Jim were inside doing paperwork, before we moved on to the customs men who could not have been more of a contrast.

In fact, it might even be fair to say that the customs guys could all have been born out of wedlock. Every single item in both vehicles was taken out and minutely inspected. This included mosquito repellent coils, which must have been seen countless times before, but each was ceremoniously taken out of its packaging, passed around, rubbed, sniffed, queried and closely examined before being given back to us to re-pack. Gerry was even more patient than Jim had been with the ferry captain and we were eventually released from their scrupulous inspection, without having to give away too many presents. We then drove through the trees, onto a beautifully smooth road and came across a huge modern complex with restaurants, villas and a hotel, all only built because Nzetzelle, where we were, was the president's home town.

Sadly, the tarmac dual carriageway ended a couple of kilometres up the road, curiously just out of sight of the president's holiday complex, but just far enough to have reached the vast red brick cathedral. Obviously missionaries, like presidents, are people you do not say no to in those parts.

The whole county was incredibly different from that on the other side of the river. The villages were noticeably friendlier and we soon knew how the British royal family must feel after constantly having to wave to the masses on ceremonial occasions.

As the climate was much more humid in the rain forests we were now driving through, we tried a variation on camping that night in a sand-scrape with a tarpaulin for a roof, tied between the two vehicles.

Sand-scrapes were where small areas of the forest had been cleared and the ground dug out for basic building materials. Normally only about the size of half a UK soccer pitch they were surrounded by dense trees and foliage and gave a sense of isolation and enclosure, but were welcome stops for vehicles and parties like ours.

That night, as we cooked our evening meal an audience of local children materialised from out of the darkness. Despite our best endeavours, they pressed ever closer until Gerry drew a line beyond which they could not go. Initial boundary success was short-lived, however, as was the sudden retreat when the pressure cooker started hissing as it let of steam.

"*Quelle horreur!*" I yelled dramatically in a hoarse whisper. "*C'est une bombe!*"

They soon came back and joined in when they heard us laughing, but gradually drifted off as the weather worsened and the storm, which had been brewing all evening, grew closer.

When it arrived, our tarpaulin roof proved to be far short of a huge success, and, as the winds raged and rains bathed down – 'bucketed' just does not seem to cover it – we made a break for it. Cutting the tarp down and relocating onto higher ground, we spent an incredibly uncomfortable night sleeping on and under each other and the camping equipment inside the vehicles.

By dawn, the rains had subsided and the crowds were back, which made Jim and Wink's early commune with nature even more uncomfortable for them both, but the audiences for both this and our breakfast were as enthusiastic and good natured as the night before. Those who were not smoking anymore were not quite as jovial as might have been expected – even after an uncomfortable night of interrupted sleep, so we packed up quickly after eating and set off into the jungle.

I have to admit that I was quite disappointed by the lack of wild nature on display in the jungle, as I had been expecting something altogether more heroic and overgrown. To my untrained eye it seemed bizarrely regular in layout and, having mulled over this fact to myself for some kilometres, I eventually broached the matter with everyone else.

"Hmm" said Charlie in a long drawn out manner – probably pondering over how to explain the situation without making me seem like a complete cretin, and then giving up, and telling me how it was. "That's because this particular stretch of jungle is actually a disused rubber plantation, as you can see from the regular right angle tracks crossing this one and the remains of that building through the trees over there!"

Once we left that unkempt environment behind and entered the real McCoy, the dense foliage had a strangely draining effect on us as there is a limited view. But at least banter in the cab was sparky as we drove down very narrow, deeply rutted earth roads with jungle spilling out from both sides, suddenly coming upon clearings with madly waving villagers, who were just as swiftly swallowed up by the vegetation again as we passed.

As time passed, the local people seemed more intent on taking a cigarette from us, or getting a present. Jim became well versed at responding "Go away-a-a-a-ay!" – the Scottish comedian, Billy Connolly's alternative to a more common phrase regarding sex and travel. He needn't have bothered, however, as we had passed a group of screaming children laughing and happily chanting "fuck off, fuck off!" – a fact which I missed until the moment was passed, having been happily waving and smiling back at them.

It was not all plain sailing, smiling and trading insults though, and as the sun set, and we searched in vain for a suitable campsite (having spurned one half an hour earlier), the fire engine slewed across the track and into the boggiest piece of ground we had encountered to date. And we got well and truly stuck up to axles in mud which could have rivalled the recipe for Super Glue.

Having reacquainted ourselves with the shovels, sand mats and the reality of being so far from home, we dug ourselves out and managed 20 minutes more travelling before becoming immobile again. This time we were less lonely and our endeavours at least provided some evening entertainment for the local villagers – who came out in force to laugh good-naturedly and cheer our every inching success as we dug, squelched, gurgled and gradually became unstuck.

By now we were very dirty, exhausted and in need of a more comfortable night and, a little further up the track, we finally found the remnants of another old plantation headquarters building and set up camp in the courtyard. Too late (and too tired to bother), we discovered that this particular sheltered site was now also serving as a local public lavatory.

**

We woke the next morning to the "oohs" and "aaahs" of jabbering children who took great delight at these nocturnal visitors as they extricated themselves from sleeping bags, sheets and mosquito nets.

It was the start of a much more damp section of the expedition and we began with a very humid (69%) and cloudy start to the day. We made good timing though, having shaken off the stickiness of the previous night, and stopped to fill up the jerry cans with fresh water at the outskirts of Bumba, a river port town with only a defunct narrow-gauge railway left to recommend it.

Again we attracted quite a crowd and Gerry and I made a pen friend with a local child called Eleve Moluka Mwatu, who smiled shyly for the camera, before asking for the biro we had used so that he could actually write to us. We never did write, but hopefully by mentioning him here I have at least helped to part honour the promise he asked from us "Make everyone at your home know me."

In the ever thickening jungle we crossed over an even more disused part of the narrow-gauge railway just south of a small town called Aketa (which no longer seems to appear on any maps) and we made camp in a little clearing by the side of the track in the middle of nowhere (again showing an unnerving lack of awareness for our surroundings as we were to discover the next morning).

The weather worsened and rained whilst I cooked supper, happily using the water as an excuse for my still abject culinary credentials when the dehydrated foods were too runny. Jim then discovered millions of ants by the food locker and so Gerry, Jamie and I became the A-Team and set about liberating the foods and destroying the attackers (life on the road had obviously got to us). Using lighter fuel as our own and pretty barbaric form of napalm, we will no doubt be brought to book at some point in the future as the event was captured on video camera with Charlie filming 'the Aketa massacre' and doing an excellent impression of a genuine war correspondent.

The video was also used to film our two visitors we had that evening. One, a praying mantis we decided to call Sid and who was destined to live in the fire engine cab with us for a while, and the other, a very intoxicated local man, who, I am pleased to say, was not.

"I smoke the cooker, I smoke the cooker" he kept repeating as he engineered himself closer to our gas rings, in what was an unusual form of greeting by our standards, but – when in Rome, and all that. We politely declined his overtures and he in turn was equally bewildered by us as a group – especially when Gerry decided to perform a striptease on top of the fire engine to the strains of Bruce Coburn signing "Who put the bullet hole in Peggy's kitchen wall?"

This is still one of my favourite songs today although maybe because of the associated imagery rather than the musical content. I cannot hear it without conjuring up the scene of us huddling together, whilst fending off a confused, drunken bushman trying to kiss our gas hob, as a normally sane young Scotsman sung his heart out and took his clothes off to the accompaniment of blue flashing lights and nature's own spectacular lightning display in the night sky. It does all somewhat add to the memory.

Later that night – as if it hadn't been eventful enough – and after a stalwart attempt at braving the elements by trying to sleep on top of the fire engine, Gerry, Wink, Jamie and myself admitted defeat and slunk back inside the vehicles. This was much to Jim and Charlie's consternation (and everyone's discomfort) – but as we closed the doors behind us, the heavens opened and I understood the true meaning of the phrase torrential downpour.

The local village by which we had unknowingly camped, and from where presumably at least one of our night time visitors had originated, came out in force the next morning to gather round and watch us wake up – something I noted would probably have happened several hours later had it not been for their noisy presence. However, with a peace offering of a bunch of bananas, we were allowed to video them and Gerry then delighted them by showing themselves on film.

The night rains had caused a few of the potentially impassable mud holes to live up to their reputations and, after an hour of slipping and sliding along the track, we were stuck fast, tilted up at an angle of 30°, with water over the back of the fire engine.

Before embarking on the trip, if I had experienced this kind of thing I would have been seriously demoralised, but Charlie had taught us well as, after all, *that's Africa babe* and Jamie simply jumped out, waded ahead in thigh-deep mud, found a stout tree and winched the fire engine out of the quagmire. As we recorded it on video (purely for the film crew and not to avoid getting dirty) we contemplated on a scale of 1-10, just how cross the film crew would be at missing this drama and unanimously gave them an 11.

The power of a winch is incredible and as it effortlessly pulled us out of the mud hole, I remembered Charlie and Gerry insisting on its installation back at John Dennis' workshops in Surrey.

"We may never even need it," said Charlie.

"Yeah, bollocks!" was Gerry's contribution to the discussion.

And having winched ourselves out it was on with the trip, driving and sliding our way down the jungle tracks until coming across a three-vehicle team lead by an ancient Mercedes van coming the other way.

"To be fair, it's all pretty good back there," they said. "There's a few shallow wallows, but no major difficulties."

I love the phrase, to be fair. It is right up there with I'm not being funny and in all honesty – completely untrue and always wrongly used as a means of conveying sincerity. And so completely appropriate here – they were almost right, but not really!

***

After a quick inspection of the vehicle it was decided that the angle of tilt was about 45° and that the mud was a third of the way up the bottom offside locker door. Not surprisingly, that was why we were stuck and why Jamie had almost fallen out of the window as we entered the mud pool. Thanks for the advice about the roads ahead, chaps.

Luckily we again winched ourselves out having dug the mud away to ease the suction, or as Jim said more thoughtfully, "Let's make it better for the next guys to come through."

Thankfully we were all too involved for anyone to video the event as we all had to hang on to the higher side of the fire engine in star jumping formation as counterbalance. Inelegant it may have been, but it worked. However, no sooner had we congratulated ourselves on a great team effort than we were faced with a smaller, but much more obviously deep hole.

We deferred to Charlie for his greater technical knowledge about overland driving in Africa and, having looked at the situation from both ends and let Gerry wade through it to quite literally test the waters, his verdict was to "go for it" – and so we did.

With a sickening, sliding motion Charlie drove the fire engine straight into the mud hole and, despite lifting the nearside front wheel clear off the ground – to the accompanying crunching, splitting sound of the fibreglass windscreen frame shattering at the top passenger side corner, leaving a gap between glass and support which you could have put a fist through – the fire engine did her stuff and went clear and it was off to Aketi. Previously known as Port Chaltin, after the Belgian officer Louis Napoleon Chaltin who fought against the arabs in the Congo Free State in the 1800s, the town had been named Aketi in 1971 following independence.

We crossed and then re-crossed the single-track railway line of the day before, which meant that at least one of us was not exactly travelling in a straight line through the overgrowth. Then we had to drive along the track and over a very narrow railway bridge to ford a rather deep gorge, luckily meeting no trains along the way.

We camped an hour out of a small town called Buta and, having learned our lessons of the previous night, put up a fly sheet and we congratulated ourselves on finding a truly deserted sand pit this time. This time it as Jim whose state of health was a cause for concern (not malaria again, but a fever none the less, but we were ever vigilant for any illness). Some years later Buta made the headlines as the centre for an outbreak of the pneumonic plague – a severe lung infection and one of the three main plagues (the others being bubonic, a lymphatic infection, and septicemic, a blood stream virus.)

**

For no real reason we had another early start and were on the road by 5.30am having been awakened by the sunlight, which seemed to be getting brighter at an earlier time each day. We later discovered that this was actually because we hadn't changed our watches at the border, but for the time being, the day had begun in hot style – 22° and 88% humidity. As the actor/comedian Robin Williams said in the newly opened movie *Good Morning Vietnam*:

"It's gonna be hot and wet! That's nice if you're with a lady, but it ain't no good if you're in the jungle."

Luckily we were aiming for another ferry crossing so there would be a cooler point coming up.

Despite the oppressive heat, we made good time and caught the ferry, and it was there that we encountered the most jobs-worth guy I have ever met. He was in charge of parking the vehicles on the ferry, which in our case with something as large as a fire engine, consisted of that and our Land Rover, but he certainly made a meal of it. He made maximum use of his whistle, which we believed was a recent Christmas present, blowing it with piercing regularity until finally he was happy and we were loaded and off – but we then had a few hiccups on the other side. The riverbank was curiously steep for a ferry exit ramp and, as Charlie tried to back onto the ferry to get a run up at the hill, the ferry moved back into the river.

There then followed one of those curious moments in life where time seemed suspended and we were in a twilight zone as our objective moved further and further away from reality. At least – until some bright spark in the engine room decided to engage the motors and push the ferry up the bank to help.

Once off we made good time and we were all set to arrive safely in Kisengani suffering no further brushes with officialdom and we were anxious to see whether we had beaten the film crew to our rendezvous to tell them of our muddy escapades.

But we had counted our blessings too early as, at that precise moment, Gerry had his film confiscated by a soldier who didn't like him photographing their dam.

"Damn!" as Jim succinctly put it.

* * *

Although Kisangani is a prime inland port, an historic town (originally named Stanleyville after Henry Morton Stanley, the English explorer who established a settlement on the nearby island some 100 years earlier), and the third largest urban area in the country, the campsite at the Hotel Olympus was not quite as grand as Charlie had promised.

We were however met by Eugene, the local wheeler-dealer Charlie had met two years earlier and who curiously said he had been expecting us. He grandly introduced us to the local Land Rover agent, a big Frenchman called Georges, whom he described as "like me, can help with all things you need." Which turned out to be quite useful.

Being only the 8th January, the no smoking brigade were not holding up well, with Gerry meeting an old friend from Nepal in a bar ("I was only giving up until Kisangani anyway") and Wink deciding that jogging in the town was probably not much safer than smoking in any event. Jim and Georges discovered a mutual interest in malt whisky and we all settled down to await the arrival of the film crew.

Departure from St Stephen's Walbrook (l-r) Jim, the author, Gerry, Ched, Wink, HRH The Duchess of Kent, Jamie, Charlie (b&w)

Jamie using the stove to prime the fire engine on a cold Swedish morning

Gerry and Jim in a campsite in northern Morocco

Chelsea not appreciating some of my cooking in the Sahara

Towing the fire engine out of soft sand in the Sahara

Taking a break from digging out the fire engine in the Sahara

The other fire engine and proof that we should not have been arrested

Wink and Gerry in the final camp at Cape Agulhas, South Africa

CHAPTER 9

The long wait – being real tourists – a new prop shaft

Unbeknown to us we were to spend seven more days as guests in the Hotel Olympus campsite waiting for the film crew to fail to arrive. However, this seemed fairly normal practice as an overland adventure travel group, led by two exceptional characters called Critter and Max, had already been there for 12 days waiting for spare parts to arrive. Bearing in mind that theirs was a paid-for trip and that several of the team had flown on to complete other parts of their itinerary, preferring to meet up somewhere later rather than wait in one place for such a long time, we were relatively unphased by the potential wait.

In many ways it was a welcome break from life on the road for us and Georges took both the fire engine and Land Rover off for a complete valeting service. He also informed us that he could make a new prop shaft for the fire engine. He then invited us all over to his house for lunch and Charlie and Jim freaked out with delight when they saw his mint condition Thunderbird parked in the driveway. Georges then proved to be even more of a hero as after eating a delicious lunch (untouched by any of our culinary hands), he gave Charlie, Jim, Wink and Jamie a lift back in the T-bird and informed us that he had booked three rooms at the hotel for us, courtesy of Land Rover, as his pleasure for being a sponsor to the expedition.

Although noisy, the air conditioning in the rooms appeared to work, so we settled down in luxury and had a holiday. Georges insisted that we all start the day with proper breakfasts and so we were forced to enjoy the hotel's facilities even more and that set the tone for our stay.

The marketplace was a goldmine of sartorial elegance and Wink found some exotically coloured material, including a English pub table cloth complete with beer branding and logos, from which she had a pair of trousers made up by local tailors. Gerry, Jamie and I preferred the more traveller-style look and had shorts made out of old jute bags.

Georges, Jim and Charlie made several fruitless trips to the airport to await the arrival of the film crew who didn't turn up. In between such trips, we established a bridge school at which I was the only pupil as the others could already play.

Bridge is a four person card game all about winning or losing tricks and our first game was begun at around 4pm one afternoon and Jim, Charlie, Jamie and I finally finished at 2am, with my game raised to the level of beginner. Jim and I seemed to play well together as did Jamie and Charlie so those were the pairings, but I noted in my diary that all three of them were hesitant to predict what I had in my hand as a result of my somewhat haphazard bidding.

As the beer flowed in one match, my bidding became even more erratic, ending up with a final game that I started with a "no bid" and second time round called "four hearts." For those like myself non-bridge players, this was bizarre bidding at its outermost limits – but worth it for the look of total incomprehension on Charlie's face, a disbelieving shake of the head from Jamie and Jim's look of naive faith. I am pleased to say that Jim and I made the tricks and won the game – but I am sure that any bridge table around the world would have winced at our approach.

On reflection, we should have been less prescriptive about the pairings as this was later to cause discontent within the team as it unfortunately and rather artlessly excluded Gerry and Wink completely, however, whilst holed up in Kisangani it worked alright.

It wasn't all games though and much work was done on the vehicles apart from just sprucing up their external appearance. Wink, Jamie and I spent one morning clearing out the fire engine's cab and lockers – finding long lost food and a box of cassettes we didn't realise we even had – while Gerry mended Charlie's windscreen mounting handiwork with the fibreglass repair kit.

"You see Jamie," said Gerry in mock schoolmasterly tones. "You have to be very precise when you mix the hardener." Two minutes later Gerry popped up onto the roof and showed Jamie a hard brown lump completely ruining the pot in which it had been mixed. "As I said, you have to be very precise. And here's one I made earlier – where I wasn't!"

Charlie and Jim also worked on the vehicles with Georges, tinkering and tweaking everything engine-wise and snugly fitting the fire engine's newly constructed prop shaft.

***

We had all formed a bond with the stranded overland group, who, after such a long time in one place, were glad of a little new company and new fireside games, but Kisangani also proved to be a meeting place for all those we had encountered on the way so far.

Two of these, Nick and Ian, driving a Land Rover sponsored by Forres School and whom we had met in Bangui arrived with a new travelling companion – a fortnight-old chimpanzee, which they had rescued from a roadside village menu board. Despite taking a leak on my shoulder, it was very cute and although not an active member of the campsite, the chimp was very quickly a firm favourite with everyone. It also proved to stimulate much debate about whether or not a rescue like this might encourage the locals to capture more live animals for a rescue sale.

Gerry and Jim both suffered bouts of intense sickness, so once again we were thankful of the beds secured by

Georges, and Wink and I experienced a different form of sickness. We discovered that the official bank exchange rate in the banks was far better than Eugene's private arrangements for dollars. Margaret Thatcher would have been proud of his entrepreneurial spirit, but I was less than impressed having trusted him and changed quite a few of my dollars.

* * *

In order not to let the grass grow too thick under our feet, Wink and I decided to check out the tourist attractions of Kisangani and left early one day to travel down the river sightseeing in a local *pirogue*, or flat-bottomed canoe, with two other English travellers, two Dutch and two Australians. It was the first real organised sightseeing we had done and it was curious to take time out to be a more traditional type of traveller, but there were plenty of sights and I wondered just how much of the world we took in travelling by road from A to B.

The deserted mosque was quite picturesque in the early light, and the rapids sparkled with excitement in the sun and we watched the Wagenya fishermen skilfully cast their nets in the waters upstream.

Upon casting, the nets fanned out into a huge circle with weighted outer edges, which then theoretically closed around the prey when pulled in again. But we had to leave that bit to our imagination as the fish were equally skilful that day, so we moved on to other fishermen trying another collecting ruse. Lifting their homemade wooden sprat traps – a bit like underwater baskets which resembled lacrosse sticks in shape – from just below the thrashing water rapids, we were thrilled to see one of them actually yield a fish. They too seemed delighted by the catch, so we presumed that they were either part of our tour guide, Philippe's, show, or fishing is a business with few rewards.

Meanwhile, Philippe's patter seemed to have a lot less to do with the business of tour guiding or fishing and a lot more to do with chatting up Wink:

"J'avais deux enfants, mais je desire me marier une autre femme," was, I thought, a particularly novel opening gambit.

After that specific tour, we joined up with others (all strangely from the Hotel Olympus campsite) and 25 of us were taken up a steep path to a small village to watch a tribal chief, in full costume, put on a some-what lacklustre show of beating his tom-toms to the accompanying rhythm of camera shutter clicks.

Many years later travelling in Bumburet in the Hindu Kush area of northern Pakistan, we travelled some distance to see a pagan festival with the same excitement, but similar disappointment – and I wondered about the real benefits of tourism.

So much for the tourist trail, but there was one more interesting sight on the agenda.

One of the overland groups was recruiting all-comers for a guided tour around the local Primus Brewery. Interest was high, which I believe had absolutely nothing to do with the promise of a free bar at the end of the tour, and, after much cajoling and arguing over available seats, 18 of us drove downtown and learned that Primus Beer was made from European hops and barley, with added rice from the Far East. Our brewery guide bravely defended the locality of his product and offered heavy protestations that it was made from "only home grown ingredients," but his arguments lost a little of their credence as he was standing on the sacks which named Thailand as their source of origin.

* * *

Our last day in Kisangani provided one of my few triumphs as provisions chief on the expedition.

One of my jobs was to ensure we had a permanent supply of clean drinking water – which when we were on the road meant filling up our big 20 litre jerry cans and adding a match head's worth of a white powder called Chloramine-T. Once dissolved in the water (the movements of a big, lumbering fire engine on unstable road surfaces provided the perfect cocktail shaker for this) it acts as a parasite control and water disinfectant. It does many other wonderful things such as kill algae formations, bacteria, fungus spores and the like, but basically it meant we could drink the water without boiling it, after letting it mix for about 15 minutes.

And here was my triumph, the pathetic nature of which offers an interesting insight into my state of mind at this juncture on the trip. I had decided to fill all our water jerry cans and performed my water purification magic in the vain hope that the film crew would arrive the next day, despite negative vibes from everyone else, so we could make a quick getaway. And that night the town's water supply went off at 1am for no apparent reason and did not come back on until the next night.

As I mentioned this was more of a pyrrhic victory (and as I remember from my history lessons at school, is named after King Pyrrhus of Epirus, who despite beating the Romans at Heraclea in 280BC suffered too many losses to be able to celebrate). By the time the water was back on, we had got word that the film crew had been refused a film permit for Zaire and that they would now not be coming to Kisangani.

Charlie hastily arranged by telex to meet one or all of them at Kigali in the neighbouring country, Rwanda, the next Sunday and then he, Wink and Jim went off to face the local and national media at a press conference arranged by the ever-resourceful Georges. The benefits of the event were not immediately apparent to our team as Charlie conducted proceedings in French, which Georges helpfully translated (back into French!), but Wink did manage to get three more offers of marriage during the course of the interviews.

"Je suis engagé," she politely declined to all overtures, whilst Charlie coughed in the background and helpfully added his own voice to the soundtrack by telling Wink not to lie about such a serious matter.

Our final evening at the Hotel Olympus was spent having a bath (after the water had been turned back on) and trying to sound interested as one of the fellow travellers from an overland group showed where he had burned a jigger off from his toe at much pain to himself, only to discover six more. I am not sure of the correct name for them, but for these pages, jiggers are small worm-like bugs which burrow under your toenails. What this said about their state of hygiene I would not like to guess, but we were at least pleasantly clean and fragrant and once again happy to have had the benefit of Georges' rooms.

CHAPTER 10

Wildlife – getting stuck – encounter with pygmies – the Equator

"7.30 am sharp for breakfast and then we are off," were Charlie's last instructions before bed, so it was with some surprise to those of us that had taken his instruction to heart (Jamie, Wink and I) when he rolled up at 8.30 am.

"Coffee," was his monosyllabic greeting as he rubbed the sleep from his eyes.

It was to be a day of departures from the Hotel Olympus campsite with almost everyone aiming to leave in the morning. Unfortunately for them I had parked the fire engine badly the night before (although pretty well for my standards) and it was casually blocking the gates to the campsite compound. So, despite Charlie's last bit of luxury in a soft bed, we still managed to be the first away at 10am and made very good time until we reached the dreaded 263 kilometre mark, at which Georges had told us there was a really muddy hole.

"It's a really big slow down for you guys," was his description.

We could have probably debated his definition once we got there, but the fact was the same – a track-wide quagmire of epic proportions.

In fact, when it was our, turn and despite not having first gear, it only took the fire engine 16 minutes to cross the mud fest. It was the two trucks in front of us who seemed to think that it was some kind of scene from a Laurel and Hardy film, slipping back and more alarmingly into the wallow with every attempt to get out. Their antics caused the several hour tailback involving six trucks on our side and five behind them coming the other way.

After watching the lorry (should I have said "Lorry and Hardy" earlier?) slip and slide around for a while, we lent them two of our sand mats. "Merci. Merci," one man shouted, before solemnly placing them at the other end of the mud bath on the solid earth of the track, while he got back down on his knees and elbows and carried on shoving branches under the wheels for better traction.

So we sat and waited and watched from our cab until, suddenly, a mere three hours later it was our turn and we were quickly and professionally through – only to find our way blocked further up the track by the previous truck who had now stalled and whose starter motor had failed. We helped its driver push it out of the way (basically into the forest) and camped half an hour down the road in a sand scrape – an area by the side of a road where earth has been dug out for use in some kind of construction process. I had picked up some kind of bug and it was now my turn to feel grim so I crashed out straight away. I note from my diary that I even avoided eating supper, which must have meant I felt really ill.

The next day proved to be a relaxed one, in terms of actual distance made, as I moaned and groaned in the Land Rover. Jim helpfully suggested a novel use for his pipe, which according to him seemed to shut me up, while the fire engine made even stranger groaning and grinding noises from underneath.

We pulled over for a quick lunch whilst Jamie popped under the fire engine. "I'm going to have a quick look at its bottom," he announced. I did not smile at this school boy humour so, although now not annoying Jim, I was still not at my normal best.

Jamie had learned his craft well and before long his head slid out from the underside of the fire engine: "Charlie. I'm no expert, but to me it looks buggered!"

On further confirmation from Charlie, the carrier bearing (a D-shaped bracket which holds the prop shaft in place) was not working harmoniously with Georges' new shaft, so an impromptu roadside engineering operation was then performed as they put the old, but now welded one from Bangui, back in place – it being thinner and able to be held by the bearing.

We made less noisy progress after that both in the Land Rover and the fire engine and eventually camped for the night just outside the city of Ubundu, on the Upper Congo River, near the spectacular Boyoma Waterfalls.

Despite the past glamour associated with Ubundu, where Humphrey Bogart, Katherine Hepburn, John Huston and the crew had stayed during the making of the classic movie *The African Queen*, we decided the waterfalls was a more restful backdrop.

Previously known as the Stanley Falls and locally called the Wagenia Falls (after the tribe we saw fishing on them), the Boyoma consists of seven sets of bubbling cascades over a 100-kilometre stretch of river and dropping some 60 metres in height.

***

Being relatively close to a wildlife reserve dedicated to protecting okapi, a rare type of brown antelope with black and white striped markings on its hind quarters and front legs, we decided to take a small detour and see some wildlife up close. We were shown around the reserve by one of the Americans who worked there and he explained that okapi are more closely related to giraffes than to antelope or the zebras they resemble. I understand that the reserve has now grown to account for about 20% of the whole Ituri Forest, the jungle through which we were travelling,

Having looked at the beautiful okapi and seen much of the other wildlife abundant on the reserve, we decided to make tracks, but were stopped at the edge of the campsite as the road had been closed for instant repairs and was not scheduled to re-open until teatime, so we settled down for a relaxed day by the river. Half an hour later however, we were told that we could go if we went immediately, so, after a mad scramble we set off again with Charlie, Jamie, Wink and I continuing our game of bridge in the fire engine.

The cards and the condition of the road made for slow progress and we were soon overtaken by two of the trucks from Kisangani, who ambushed us as they passed, attacking with water pistols when we wound down the windows to wave.

Shortly after that we met up with an Encounter Overland trip coming north and, as Charlie and Gerry knew the leader, Kevin, we decided to follow them back up the road and camp with them. His group were fairly subdued and quiet so we added some welcome relief to proceedings with some *haute cuisine* (soup à la Gerry, followed by corn beef hash and avocado vinaigrette à la Jim) – or so we thought. We were a little shame-faced when they produced freshly made chocolate pudding and custard, but, being rugged travellers around a campfire, there was only one thing to do. We swapped recipes.

Earlier that night Gerry had organised for one of the local pygmies to clear our campsite with his machete and he invited Gerry and I to see his own nearby encampment.

He was one of the traditional nomadic pygmy hunters from what sounded like the Mbuti tribe and they proved to be incredibly hospitable. After a couple of hours of lively chatter, but not altogether common understanding, we had been most generously looked after and it was time for us to leave – and to discover that we all had the same slapstick sense of humour.

Luckily it was Gerry, who is a little shorter than I am, but still stood a good head and shoulders above our hosts, stood up first to leave the hut and cracked his forehead on the top of their doorway. They did perhaps learn a few new Anglo Saxon terms from us, but we parted the happiest of friends and with their laughter ringing in our ears.

* * *

The next morning we passed through a village that we had been through twice the night before, much to the locals' bemusement, and we made good time along the roads which appeared marginally drier and therefore considerably better. We also played the helpful traveller on two occasions, using our winching kit to assist two stranded trucks. For the record, there was no truth in the rumour that we would have driven past had there been any passing space on either side, but as darkness fell, it was our turn to fall foul of the bogs and typically, we were alone at the time.

Earlier in the afternoon, Jim in the Land Rover had given the fire engine a tow up a steep hill and over a particularly deep hole, which without first gear had proved to be a major obstacle. So, as darkness fell, we decided to try the same approach when faced with an extremely deep muddy wallow. We were half way around the edge of it when the fire engine's nearside rear wheels slipped off the bank and we performed a repeat of the stuck-in-the-mud game from a couple of weeks earlier – except that this time the 45° list was the other way, treating the contents of the lockers on the other side of the fire engine to a mud bath.

Having elegantly descended into the mud hole, we then became immovable due to a submerged rock which became wedged in front of the back wheels. The rock may have previously helped some other luckless driver, but it was a distinct hindrance to us. Still, one of the benefits of driving through jungle is that there are plenty of trees around which winch cables can be fastened. So, by using a conveniently stout jungle tree trunk and the Land Rover as two fulcrums, the full length of both vehicles' winch cables (operating simultaneously) and with Gerry, Wink, Jamie and I balanced precariously in our star jump formations on the upturned side for ballast, we managed to free ourselves with a deep sucking splurge.

I am not sure that I had ever considered the possibility of taking nearly two hours to get out of a hole as a realistic probability on the trip, still there we were and that is what it took.

Despite the darkness, we were greatly cheered by the local crowd of spectators who had as usual emerged seemingly from nowhere to monitor our progress and so, although on our own, we were at least not alone. And the final sucking gurgle as we emerged from the mud was particularly satisfying for everyone concerned.

The next morning while cooking breakfast, Gerry and I became aware of a hushed noise behind us and ended up cooking for not just the team, but the local children who had begun a game of grandmothers footsteps with us as they crept forward to see what we were cooking. Every time we turned round they nonchalantly pretended to be studying the fire engine but were a step closer each time.

* * *

Having had so much fun in the mud the day before, we decided to take more care and actually film things should that happen again. We took many minutes of footage of both vehicles slipping and veering off the track in strange directions, but we were soon in luck – and managed to completely bog the fire engine down in the most innocuous looking pool of muddy brown water.

It was like one of those puddles you might see in a slapstick film where an Elizabethan noble might lay down his cloak over the mess for a lady to step on and when she does so, she promptly sinks without trace.

In this specific instance the sides of the water-hole were very steep and we got some great footage of our double winch manoeuvre from the day before and a great recording of the fire engine's twisted frame causing

Jamie and Gerry's fibreglass repair to splinter open again with a crack like a pistol shot.

But we were at least making progress and at 8.30am, we crossed over the Equator and marked the event by getting out of the vehicles and spitting on the ground at both sides. I am assured that this is the correct procedure, however, being my first time I had no reference point. I have since crossed the Equator a number of times in both Africa, South America and Indonesia and been considerably more traditional in my celebrations, preferring to watch water drain out of a bucket with the eddy going in the opposite direction. At this juncture in my life, however, I was impressionable and did what I was told.

In the Southern Hemisphere, the roads improved and we made good progress motoring along and surprising another overland group who, having pulled up at the side of the track, were thus stationary. They proved an easy target for our flour bombs, which Gerry feverishly created in paper bags in the fire engine cab and we threw through their lorry. Again, this was apparently a tradition to which I had been blissfully unaware in my previously sheltered life as an insurance broker.

Soon we arrived at a huge mud hut village that seemed to sprawl on forever before us. In his best tour guide tones, Charlie informed us:

"This African village, inhabited by the Banande people, is the largest such village in the world."

To which a voice in the back suspiciously sounding like Jamie's enquired, "Is it the largest one in Africa then?"

Deciding to concentrate on the village rather than speak, we drove on through and it was the most unbelievable sight. Mud houses stretched over every hill we crested and as far again off to the sides. One house I noted was a magnificently constructed two-story affair, complete with central door and two windows on the top floor, exactly mirroring the one beneath, but with apparently with no stairs up to the first floor.

At length we had passed through the village and we entered the Parc National des Virunga for some big game viewing – and we were not disappointed. We saw our first eland, or giant eland as I should probably say – the largest species of antelope in the world – and two magnificent hippopotami (both vegetarian animals, but as my first real taste of African wildlife, both quite scary and large).

Despite having been back to many African countries since this trip, and been lucky enough to see the big five on multiple occasions – or safari grand slams as Charlie called them (buffalo, elephant, leopard, lion and rhinoceros) – I can watch wildlife for ages without getting remotely bored.

Africa's first national park and designated a World Heritage site in the late 1970s by UNESCO, the Virunga National Park has, as a wildlife haven, survived almost despite itself. Civil war, genocide, retreating refugee influxes, poaching, military invasion and staff being ousted through guerilla activity should have meant the end. But today the park survives and so I am told by recent visitors, it is actually thriving. As are the gorillas (the correct type for such a place rather than the armed militia), which, although we never saw, are still in abundance on the Rwandan side.

But for us and before most of those tribulations hit it, Virunga managed a surprise of its own as we discovered when we checked in at the middle checkpoint. The guards informed us that the park was closing and that we should have to stay the night at their lodge (30,000 Zaires for the group and vehicles for one night – which from my memory was about US$15,000.)

"Tenting and *slipping* on your own is not allowed here."

This caused a slightly awkward scenario as we had nowhere near that amount of cash on us as we were aiming for the border and Zaires, the local currency, were of no use anywhere other than this country. Bearing in mind the border was not far from the other side of the park, we had purposefully spent what we had and no intention of being saddled with useless funny money.

"We have no money at all," said Jim, adopting an elder statesman-like approach. "Tenting and *slipping* was our plan."

"OK," said the much put out guard. "No monies - you must leave now. No stops before the gates. No tenting. No *slipping*. Go and make fast."

We promised to do just that and were finally allowed to go on our way (with no tenting or *slipping*) only to stop half a kilometre later to look at some more hippos. Having taken our fill of them we returned to the present and sped off to the park gates, where we were greeted by some exceptionally grumpy guards. After a brief display of jobs-worth and questions as to how we could have such a fine red vehicle but no money, they let us out.

Where upon we promptly tented and *slipped* in the bushes just outside their post.

CHAPTER 11

Rendezvous – luxury – malaria

Following an early start and in anticipation of tarmac roads in Rwanda, we covered the 70 kilometres distance to Goma without incident, reaching the airport and the smooth black roads at around mid-morning.

Goma is on the northern shore of the beautiful Lake Kivu and where we were to cross the border into the neighbouring Rwandan city of Gisenyi. Six years after our arrival, Goma was the scene of several atrocities in the Rwandan Genocide of 1994 and eight years after that much of the city was destroyed by the eruption of the Nyiragongo Volcano to its north.

But in 1988, all was peaceful and the city was thriving and streets filled with happy people, including Wink's mother and sister, Grania, who were soon to go off on a gorilla-watching trip. We just had time for Grania to say that we could stay with her when we got to Johannesburg, when we were approached by a manic girl from Devon who had left Critter's overland trip in Kisangani and was desperate to meet up with them again.

"Where is he? Are you from Devon? Isn't this fire engine great? Any room?" and a million other questions were all asked in the same breath. Jamie tried to placate her with the news that Critter was in front of us, but it sent her into a fresh fervour:

"Oh! My! God! Oh my God! We've missed him! Oh my God where is he? Oh my God what am I going to do?" etc.

We left her "Oh my God-ing" with her fellow trip escapee and set off for the border post and to meet up with the film crew, whom Grania had bumped into in Gisenyi.

We were all a little apprehensive at the checkpoint as we knew that delay had meant that our entry visas had now expired, but we were pleased to discover that our film director, Graham, had left a photo of the fire engine and an explanatory letter at the Rwandan side of the border post. Maybe because of that, or just a more *laissez-faire* attitude, the Rwandan guards were pretty relaxed and they stamped our passports without much questioning or inspection and it was on to the Meridian Hotel for the rendezvous with the film crew.

As one of our sponsors, the manager of the Meridian fixed us up with free rooms and we, in turn, repaid his kindness by washing off much of the last few weeks' mud and grime to present an altogether more appropriate spectacle in the lobby as we caught up on news.

Lake Kivu is one of the African Great Lakes and acts as part of the border between the modern day Democratic Republic of Congo and Rwanda. Almost 1,500 metres above sea level and covering around 2,700 square kilometres, the waters are part of the East African Rift valley, making it very deep in places (over 480 metres). Nestled in amongst lush green mountains it is spectacularly beautiful and was, I mused, presumably named after some such vision.

"Nah," said John, one of the hotel waiters when I mentioned this later. "Kivu means lake in Bantu, the local language here."

Regardless of its naming origins and unable to resist the allure of its stunning waters, Jim and I went for a sail while Gerry and Graham went out for some windsurfing. For a semi-professional sailor such as Jim and a complete novice such as me, Jim was one of the most patient teachers I have ever had, and the afternoon lazed by – in complete contrast to our hard work in the mud wallows of the previous few days. That evening, sound man Tim recorded a local minstrel singing his version of *Jambo Bwana* (Swahili for *hello mister*) – a classic tune from our Kisangani days and one which would happily feature on the soundtrack to the final edit of the film.

* * *

All was not rest and relaxation though, as we then had to catch up on some filming work and spent the whole of the next day shooting forest/jungle shots. We even managed to find some authentic bumpy tracks and a few mud holes in which we deliberately bogged ourselves down – a process that proved to be much harder to do when intentional.

We allowed ourselves one more lazy start, swimming in the lake before breakfast and trying out a diving board from the end of the jetty, neither of which looked especially safe. Jim had his longest interview session on camera to date and we all prolonged our tasks of readying the vehicles, but despite this, we finally left what was probably the best campsite in the world and were back on the road by lunch.

The Rwandan scenery was breath-taking and after more filming we stopped for an impromptu picnic by yet another glorious waterfall. Watched by an ever-growing group of locals who continued to emerge from the foliage, the event was slightly marred by a thoroughly unpleasant odour which seemed to follow us around. After some investigation the source happily proved not to be my feet again – unfortunately for Jamie (who was almost sick on discovery) but happily for us, it was a tray of broken three-week-old eggs in the rear fire engine locker that was the culprit.

After clearing up the pungent eggs and filming more footage for the documentary, it was back onto the tarmac at Gitarama, Rwanda' second-largest city and the principal gateway to the south and west of the country. Our destination was Rwanda's capital city of Kigali – for yet another soft night of camping with our sponsor, Meridian Hotels – where we were greeted rather incongruously by the strains of Monty Python's *Always Look on the Bright side of Life*, showing on the video in the hotel lobby. I again slept like the dead and noted in my diary how tiring it was even just pretending to be a film star.

Located almost in the geographic centre of Rwanda, Kigali has been the nation's capital since it gained independence in 1962. It was also the scene of the Rwanda genocide massacre in 1994 when almost one million local Tutsu people were killed by Hutu militia and members of the national army. Although rebuilt now and largely back to full strength as a city, I remember watching pictures of the devastation on TV back in the UK and seeing the eye-catching ruins of the Meridien Hotel where we had stayed.

But for us, Kigali proved to be slow and relaxed and we spent two days there during which we were telexing madly for permission to film in Tanzania – our next destination – while simultaneously trying to get someone to give us visas to actually get there ourselves.

However, with our passports left in the embassy, and in driving rain, Gerry and I went off to the market for provisions. Jim, our paymaster, was a little low on cash at that precise moment so he gave us strict shopping instructions:

"If it is a choice between Coke and a packet of ciggies – then get the ciggies!"

Luckily we proved to be more adept at shopping than Gerry was in the restaurant where we he and I went for lunch that day – having ordered what he thought was a chicken dish, he was lovingly presented with fish. Having dined and, more importantly replenished our supplies we were at least ready for the off once the visas were sorted.

Lawrence, Graham's friendly man at the Ministry of Tourism, had phoned earlier about the Tanzanian visas, but, due to the strong influence of alcohol had proved incoherent. He rang again later that evening in a better state and advised us that all papers were in order and that he would accompany us to the border at 8am the next morning, so we packed up and watched a video in the hotel that night.

Very excitingly, my sister, Ginny, rang through to the hotel from London to say that she had given birth to her second child earlier that day and that I now had a new nephew, Harry, to come home to.

* * *

As promised, Lawrence turned up the next morning at 8.30am, not looking too much the worse for wear, and he lead the way to Tanzania at a hair-raising pace – with the Land Rover and the film crew in hot pursuit. The fire engine languished around in town to buy some fresh chickens and fill up with diesel. This was not due to the previous day's supplies shopping trip being inadequate – it was all in the interests of filming so that Graham could get some shots of it crossing the border.

This cunning plan was unfortunately foiled when we got there as the border was closed, so we stopped for lunch in the shelter of a previous road accident involving three lorries and a petrol tanker, hastily changing some cash with one of the many black market men who in those days were a common site at African borders and always ready to do a deal for US dollars. This one was alarmingly within sight of the Tanzanian side, so the shillings were actually hidden on Gerry for safety – the money was safe and for the rest of the day he experienced a feeling of being rather heavily endowed:

"It's not a sensation with which I am unfamiliar," he assured us.

The guards were specially pernickety and were not pleased that our visas for Rwanda had expired and not impressed that we had no Rwandan money left to appease the situation. Bizarrely, they were happy for Gerry to jog back to the shelter of the road accident and then return (miraculously now with the right money) so that we could pay for a few hours' worth of extensions.

One Tanzanian guard made an issue of the amount and variety of cameras, but all problems were solved once Graham showed him our telexed permission to film in their country, which he soberly and laboriously read through, word for word, before languidly waving us through. It wasn't until he had handed the document back that Graham noticed that the paper he'd given him referred to free meals at the Meridian Hotel in Kigali. In any event, it had impressed him and done the trick and we left the border guards squabbling over the sharing out of a packet of Polo mints.

Having camped off the side of the road in a sand scrape, we breakfasted with some workmen who had arrived the night before to dig truckloads of sand from their quarry (where we were sleeping) and set off on the relative smoothness of tarmac, but heading towards some amazingly ominous black clouds that were rolling and swirling dangerously in the distance.

More immediately though, the tarmac ended at a sort of inspection post which consisted of a barrier arm across the road in a makeshift fashion, and a not very clear indication of what was required from us. The young chap reclining in his office chair as we came to a halt leapt up and stuck his head through the window. "Have you any *smokeys* for me?" he asked.

Having completed the formal paperwork (one *smokey* gratefully received by him), he let us pass and it was back onto the dirt roads again – this time more sandy orange than muddy so an altogether more colourful experience.

Graham decided to take a close-up shot of the fire engine going through a puddle so he and John settled down by the edge of some obliging water and set up their equipment as we reversed the fire engine back down the track. Tim realised what may have been afoot and took up position with his sound boom on the other side of the road. John waved the signal to proceed. Charlie put his foot down and the fire engine's wheels created the perfect surfer's wave from the puddle which completely drenched the camera, Graham and John.

Coincidentally, it was a natural place to stop for lunch, so while we ate and tried to coax a small smile from

Graham and John (who strangely hadn't seen the funny side of it), they took the Aaton 16mm camera apart to clean and dry it and did the same for themselves.

Graham's camera of choice for this picture, the Aaton LTR 16mm, was specifically designed for use in the field, such as for documentaries, and it featured a time code signal on the margin of each frame for highly accurate audio synchronization back in the editing suite. To me it also seemed highly complicated to strip down, clean and dry, but Graham was relatively unfazed by this and still happy with his choice.

Having eaten, cleaned and dried, we then discovered that the Land Rover had another flat tyre – it was the one which the man from Bangui had 'mended' – so, until we could get to a garage, it was a question of driving with our fingers crossed and not getting another one, at least until we reached some form of civilisation. This was, in fact, the next day after we made good time to Lake Victoria and serendipitously found that the ferry was about to come in. So we had a very hasty lunch and then had to wait 40 minutes before they would let us on board.

Named in honour of his queen by John Speke, who was the first European to discover it, Lake Victoria is another of the seven African Great Lakes – but unlike Lake Kivu, is relatively shallow, with an average depth of only around 40 metres. It is absolutely massive though and, with a surface area of just shy of 69,000 square kilometres, it is not only Africa's largest lake, but also the world's largest tropical lake.

The ferry journey over our section of it was short and soon we were back on the road and reached Mwanza on the southern shores of the lake where we stopped to fill up on fuel and food in the market-place. Gerry was feeling a bit grim so he and I stayed in the fire engine whilst the others went off to the market with an old friend of Charlie's, who promised to take them to the 'best value stall around' – which coincidentally was also his brother-in-law's.

Within five minutes of everyone having left us, Gerry was in deep trouble and I was getting scared. He was experiencing great difficulty in breathing, having hot and cold flushes and screaming at me to clear away hoards of imaginary black spiders off both him and the walls of the cab, while thrashing around fitting on the floor of the cab.

Pathetically I had no idea what to do so I turned on the fire engine's sirens and repeatedly pushed the horn while talking calmly to Gerry and trying to reason with him about the spiders. Luckily Charlie, who had in fact not been too far away from the fire engine when the sirens went, off came back and after a quick look at Gerry, ran to get a doctor, who by another amazing piece of good fortune, he had just met in the market. After a brief, visual medical diagnosis, we drove to a nearby clinic and tried to prise Gerry out of the fire engine cab and into the consulting room.

Gerry is pretty strong at the best of times, but in his feverish delirium he was even more so, and he pulled and resisted every move we made, twisting and trying to escape as Charlie, Jamie and I strong-armed him out of the fire engine cab and into the clinic.

"No needles!" he kept screaming – even in his delirious state he was aware enough of his surroundings and predicament to be nervous of potential further infection through use of unsterilized equipment.

The film crew had followed in hot pursuit in the Land Rover (except for John, who having missed the vehicle had to run the few hundred yards to the clinic) and we settled Gerry down on a bench to have a blood test taken. He calmed down a little once outside the close confines of the fire engine cab – even when the nurse tried to take his temperature by placing a glass thermometer under his tongue. He was soon ready for us to take him to the main hospital to be treated for what the doctor suspected was cerebral malaria.

Despite taking preventative medicines, the disease is prevalent with many variants throughout the region. Cerebral malaria is a particularly severe form of the infection and, normally showing signs after around ten days' incubation, it can be fatal if not treated early enough. Luckily, Gerry was being treated within moments of developing the signs of the disease so whilst very scary, we were thankful for the location in which we were.

A bed was found for him at the end of a ward, as the incumbent was unceremoniously lifted out of it, put on a sheet on the floor and then carried away by two orderlies. Charlie later surmised that the man had unfortunately already passed away in the bed, but tactfully refrained from telling Gerry this until some days later. We left Jim, Charlie and the film crew with Gerry in the hospital while Jamie, Wink and I went back to guard the fire engine in the hospital car park.

As was now wholly predictable on the trip, a crowd of children rapidly gathered around us, fascinated by the fire engine and were jumping up and tapping on the windows, laughing and screaming through the glass.

"Cigarette Mister?" "Missy, Missy. Have you a pen for me?" etc.

After about 45 minutes of this constant onslaught the door behind Wink suddenly opened and so it was not altogether unwarranted of me to sternly tell the intruder to go away (using the well-known phrase referring to sex and travel.) Unfortunately though, the impeccably dressed, middle-aged chap who had opened the door was visibly shocked and could not have looked more surprised.

"You cannot be serious?" he stammered. "I do not believe that in my whole life I have ever been spoken to in such a rude manner."

After hasty apologies and explanations that we had mistaken him for one of the children, the Director General of the hospital politely asked us to move the fire engine as it was blocking the main entrance. I have rarely been so embarrassed by my behaviour and, on reflection, couldn't really believe that I would have said this to one of the children either, but was not pondering for long as shortly afterwards the guys came out.

To no-one's surprise, Gerry needed to stay in hospital so Charlie elected to spend it with him having established our campsite and a plan for the morning. Camping in town was a new experience and we stopped nearby the hospital in what may have been a public meeting ground – in any event, the two thatched rotunda-type buildings became very nice cabanas.

The next morning dawned bright and sunny and the news from the hospital was the same when Jim and I arrived to pick up Charlie. Gerry had responded well to the drugs and, incredibly, would be able to leave with us after lunch. Jim stayed with Gerry and we packed up our camp. Wink did an interview to camera and Charlie and Jamie took the fire engine to a local garage, which Charlie knew of old, with some more technical instructions.

"See if you can get them to tart it up a bit."

I then took Graham and Wink into town to finish the interrupted shopping from the day before, fill up with water and pick up Gerry and Jim. The Director General did not look best pleased to see me again following our previous conversation and we then further upset him when Graham started filming in his hospital. However, after a schoolmaster/naughty schoolboy type confrontation in his office, we were allowed to leave quietly – with our patient.

Gerry was looking and feeling much better, although slightly confused following a curious chat with the doctor who had treated him the night before, but who seemed, by his totally weird account of it, to have been slightly more delirious than Gerry himself.

And so it was with some relief that, having met up with the others, we left Tanzania's second largest city behind us. Eternally grateful that Gerry had taken ill in such a modern, well-equipped place, we set off for the contrasting tranquillity of the Serengeti – 30,000 square kilometres of ecological open space and home to the world's largest annual animal migration.

We made such good time on the tarmac roads that Jim, in the Land Rover, had trouble keeping up at times and we camped about 90 kilometres from the Serengeti National Park at an ideal flat and sheltered site. We put the tents up for the first time since Tamanrasset in the Sahara and got on with the evening chores and life as we had known it on the road.

Unfortunately, while cutting up onions something flew into my eye and I instinctively wiped it out with my finger, thus transferring the onion juice. In an effort to appease the pain, I tipped a mug of water into it and Gerry was overheard quietly asking me: "And just exactly how long have you had a drink problem, Jules?" We were back to normal.

CHAPTER 12

Big cats – Pope-mobiles – the Maasai

Our campsite turned out not to be as ideal as we first thought. When we were awakened by the noise of crops being crushed and ground on the rocks all around us. We had set up home in a factory.

So, having been woken early and partly in an effort to leave Jim and Wink's puns behind ("Wheat a minute," "Corn I have a cup of tea?" and "A-maize-ing" being about the best), we set off shortly after dawn.

As we approached the Serengeti National Park, full of anticipation and excitement for seeing a David Attenborough-style programme in real life (well I was at any rate), the Land Rover developed another puncture. This was a problem because, due to the distractions of our recent dramas, the spare tyre was still flat. The incident provided great hilarity for most of us though as John was having his first go at driving at the time and failed to see the entertainment value of the video that Tim and I made, using the fade button to imply that the puncture had taken two days to fix. In reality, Jim merely pumped up the spare, which had only a slow puncture, and set off in the lead only to disappear in a cloud of dust about ten kilometres later as the fire engine coughed, spluttered and then stopped on a hill.

Amidst the same sort of noises we had heard in the Sahara when this had last happened and, following some frantic pumping, Charlie realised that we had just run the main tank dry – my fault as driver, of course (which is probably true as I have done this quite regularly since).

"There Jules. That's quite a good gauge to keep an eye on now and again."

We switched tanks and it wasn't long before we were back on the road, which possibly by the proximity of wildlife, or the appearance of some latent East End of London characteristics, Charlie now insisted on calling the *frog & toad* in cockney rhyming slang.

The word Serengeti is from the Maasai word, *serengit*, which literally means 'endless plain', and the National Park is arguably the jewel in its crown. It is certainly Tanzania's most famous game park. Covering an area of slightly less than 15,000 square kilometres, the Serengeti National Park is probably most famous for the annual zebra and white-bearded wildebeest migration involving around two million of these animals. In addition it hosts a vast array of bountiful game, including its own big five (so named after the five most prized trophies for hunters of days gone by): black rhinoceros, buffalo, elephant, leopard and, of course, lion.

Not long after our trip, the authorities recognised the potential harm to the parks by having loads of people driving their own cars around wherever they pleased, not to mention another revenue stream, and they decided to close the national parks to private vehicles. You can now only tour around them by authorised vehicle and guide, which I am sure is just as exciting, but we certainly felt the freedom to move wherever we wanted to was a huge addition to the overall impact of the experience. I have also read recently of plans to build a road through part of the park – for which I am sure they have their reasons.

Within the first hour it was as if we had been watching a wildlife special, with animals appearing on cue, and we saw giraffe, gazelle, warthogs, topis (a kind of antelope), maribou storks, eagles and a cheetah. As the latter came out of the bush a mere five metres in front of the fire engine, we stealthily followed it for a while – in as much that a huge bright red, several ton fire engine can be stealthy.

We then struck animal gold, which took me a few minutes to realise as I was leaning over on one side of the fire engine's roof studying a dung beetle rolling a ball twice its own size along the rutted track. Everyone was flat against the other side of the roof looking at a pride of lions with their young cubs less than three metres away from the fire engine. Having elected to travel in the fire engine, Graham was in an emotional turmoil.

"I hope it's this good when I've got my ruddy camera with me!" he muttered.

In the late afternoon we drove to the Seronera Lodge where we arranged to pitch camp on their site. Jim and Charlie fixed the Land Rover's tyres and found that the man from Bangui had left the end of a nail in the outer tread and it was this which had caused the second puncture in almost the same place as the last mend.

That evening around the fire we took full advantage of our Agfa sponsorship (they had provided us with a variety of 35mm print and slide film stock) and took photos of some spectacular distant lightning. Everyone was convinced that we would all be fighting off advances from National Geographic Magazine for our work, but sadly this proved to be an unsolicited conviction quickly dismissed when we had the pictures developed. After the trip, my father's only comment on my supposedly award-winning series of prints was "I hope you didn't pay for all that film!"

That evening I was awoken by a sort of grunting, guttural snorting sound and happily thought "That's Africa babe" as I rolled over in my sleeping bag and went back to sleep. The next morning we discovered that Charlie had had a fitful night, having heard a lion prowling around the campsite and been in a state of alert for the duration. For me at least, I could prove the old saying – ignorance really is bliss.

***

Having risen early on our first Serengeti morning and digested Charlie's news, looked at the lion's paw prints and eaten a quick snack for breakfast, we set off in high spirits for some real ecotourism to find some wildebeest, or white-bearded gnus (as they are also known). I am not sure now why we had to rise so early to find them as their numbers were vast and they spread out over the plane like a moving brown carpet, interspersed with huge numbers of black and white zebra. On closer inspection we discovered that most zebra are, in fact, more brown than black but the Attenborough-esque image called for black and white animals.

Although not as dramatic as when they are migrating, they still stretched as far as the eye could see and Graham and John got some great footage of us driving carefully through the herds. In amongst the vast numbers we also saw hyena and jackals, but despite causing minor unrest we did not witness a proper stalking, so Graham resorted to my enthusiasm of the previous day and intently filmed a dung beetle's attempts at rolling a ball of wildebeest turd.

Also curiously among the wildlife throngs were several 'Pope mobiles', as we called them. These white coloured, official game-viewing cars, which looked quite similar to the cars which carry round the pontiff on official tours, came streaming in from every which way towards any vehicle which had stopped in the hope of seeing something of specific excitement. We soon learned that by stopping a long way away, they would soon notice us and flock over to view whatever it was which had proved so arresting to us. We then hot-tailed it out of there to see some real sights. Probably another good reason for not allowing private cars into the park these days, but we mainly wanted to avoid the tourists inside following an early encounter when a loud, penetrating American female voice hailed us asking "Are you guys all from Britland?"

As we approached Lake Lagaja to stop for lunch, there was great excitement as Jamie and I thought that we had spotted the rarest cat of all, a leopard. Fever pitch quickly abated, however, as sadly it turned out to be a nest with a creeper hanging down from the tree branch.

Lake Lagaja is one of two shallow soda lakes in the park, which are formed in natural land hollows from surface water run-off. They dry out in the hot season leaving salty encrustation on the earth from the minerals such as calcium, sodium and potassium, which are concentrated into the lakes from the surface soil run off water when they fill up. Apart from being home to flamingos ("both Greater and Lesser types," Charlie sagely informed us), we were surrounded by thick clouds of big black flies. This made eating rather adventurous – and so in true hardy traveller style we decided that we should head for Lobo Lodge that night, up in the north of the park some five hours' drive away.

In the scrubland along the way and shortly after Seronera, Jamie spotted two male lions within ten yards of the road so we stopped again for more big cat watching and curious conversation between Wink and Charlie:

"Is it safe to go outside?"

"No."

"To get some cigarettes from one of the side lockers?"

"Yes. Definitely!"

After some more shutter clicking we set off and made good time to the lodge where Charlie bought supper and we revelled in being the only people staying there. I am told that this too is now an almost impossible feat – which is good news for them I suppose. Recent events caught up with Gerry and he went to bed early absolutely exhausted and accidentally managed to lock Jim out of their room. Despite Jim yelling through the door, ringing Gerry on the room's phone and knocking heavily on the window, the manager had to be called with a spare key and even then Gerry was blissfully oblivious to the world.

***

The restful lie-in we had anticipated, being the only lodge guests, was sadly to be postponed by Gerry who, apart from being unaware of the treat was now refreshed by a long sleep and was wide awake at 5.30am. As he said later, "I was forced to pinch Charlie's nipples which were titilatingly revealed by the sheet" and this was our undoing. Charlie leapt out of bed yelling "Not my nipples!" at the top of his voice, disturbing the peaceful slumber of everyone else and possibly most of the wildlife and so we all found ourselves assembled for breakfast in the restaurant, on our rest day, when it opened at 8am.

Considering we were ostensibly on a mission during the trip, it might seem strange to have a rest day in such luxurious surroundings, but we were working well as a team and getting on well as a group and keen to add some human life to the documentary, so we made the most of it and the facilities.

The morning progressed with a hectic and often wildly erratic game of Frisbee from which there were two minor casualties – Jim, whose nose was sliced by an errant throw from Jamie and me, whose middle toes were savaged by a rogue flip-flop made from some old car tyre, which made me question again the sensibility of such footwear. Meanwhile, Wink was sitting on a rock and sewing to the appreciation of the camera (a highly contrived set up), while Gerry and Charlie, once more bosom buddies, relaxed by the pool.

And then the rains came down and we were forced into the bar for card games and a new form of darts called Killers. Each person picks a number on the dartboard and tries to hit it three times with their darts. On achieving three hits, you become a Killer and can wipe out other players' scores by hitting their numbers. The winner is the last person playing. Having taught us all how to play, Jamie was promptly out on the first round and retired complaining good-naturedly about blunt darts.

As quickly as they had started, the rains stopped and, although the light wasn't good, we went out for a game drive and almost immediately came across two lionesses, who being much put out and very camera shy, ran out of sight behind a *kopje*.

Kopjes (pronounced copy, and technically known as inselbergs) are outcrops of granite rock whose surface has been weathered and eroded into rough boulders and stones. Normally covered in vegetation they stand out like small mountains rising out of the African plains. So it wasn't surprising that having driven round the other side of this one we had lost our prey. In the effort to relocate them, John, who was driving the Land Rover, took an alternative route and promptly got stuck up to the axles. Making matters worse he tried to winch himself out via two large rocks, but by the time we came around in the fire engine, he was still stuck fast with two newly dislodged boulders for company. We towed the Land Rover out, however, not only had we made far too much noise for watching wildlife, we again didn't have a camera to record this.

The next day we decided on a more professional approach and we began bright and early at 6.30am, filming a troop of baboons feeding on the top of the fire engine. Within ten minutes we came across a hole in the road which we filled with nearby rocks, basically rebuilding the road, and then another a few minutes later which we could not refill as it went right through an overhang beneath!

We scanned the horizon for wildlife, which the rains (rather than us) seemed to have scared off, but shortly we became the focus of the photography from a nearby Popemobile, when the fire engine needed the Land Rover to give it a tow up a particularly slippery slope. After some more natural hazards, including one in which Graham began filming from the Land Rover's bonnet and ended up still filming, but from within the mud hole we were trying to circumvent, we came to a small Maasai settlement, or *enkaji*, were we stopped to view a way of life unchanged for generations.

Historically a semi-nomadic people, Maasai settlements are designed for easy transportation and are enclosed in a circular fence usually made of thorned acacia with a corral in the middle for increased protection of their animals at nighttime. Using readily available materials, their houses are normally circular, with timber support poles set into the ground, lattice-woven with smaller branches, and then plastered with a mix of mud, grass, cow manure, ash and urine to ensure waterproofed rooves.

Our settlement was typical of this corral style and, although basically tourists, we were at least able to be of some use, with Wink and Gerry treating a small boy who had a nasty burn on his arm and hand with our medical supplies.

Having left the Maasai, we continued along the tracks and were forced to put the ice chains, last used in Finland, on the tyres as the mud was almost oil-like in consistency. It was also exceedingly smelly, which did add to the ambiance inside the vehicles after getting stuck again in one cesspool of a wallow. And for the second time in 24 hours, the fire engine had to tow the Land Rover.

Having reached dryer ground, we were taking the chains off and suddenly became aware of a lone visitor – a Maasai whom we discovered had not spurned the western world completely after he managed to persuade John to part with his watch in return for some filming.

"That's the last time I give a Maasai a watch," he said putting away the camera, but was happy as our visitor had demonstrated amazing presence and looked magnificently incongruous against the backdrop of the two vehicles in his traditional red, black and white hooped decorated clothing.

Having watched our friend wander off into a seemingly deserted distance, we drove down the other side of the hill and were half way up again when the fire engine slid off to the edge of the road. Being incredibly heavy and a dead weight, the sideways motion of the big red beast was quite alarming as we appeared to have had no way of missing Jim in the Land Rover who was frantically spinning his own wheels just in front. Luckily we did miss him, but the camber of the hill was such that it was very hairy tow, with a semi-broadside fire engine crabbing up the hill behind the straining Land Rover.

Some years later, David Henriques and I came across a magnificent expression which would have amply described Jim's predicament as the fire engine slid towards him. Speaking to Hector, a giant of a Scottish lobster fisherman on the Isle of Tiree, about an episode in a ferocious storm when he had had to jump over the side of his boat and hold it off from the rocks single-handedly for almost an hour before help came.

"Were you scared, Hector?" asked David.

"Nae lad," he replied with a mischievous twinkle in his eye. "But ma arse was twitchin."

Having finally reached the top and unharnessed the vehicles, we had all had enough and set up camp amidst howling winds and driving rain, which had in some way helped us decide to call it a night. It was then that Gerry discovered that the tomato purée we'd bought in Kigali was in fact red hot-pepper purée. Too late for alternatives, we had a fairly hot meal which really warmed us from within.

* * *

We set off the next morning and within 20 yards of the campsite the fire engine was stuck broadside across the road having slalomed its way into position. The Land Rover, obviously unaware of what the mirrors were for and totally oblivious to the our plight, skated on regardless, returning a quarter of an hour later after we had managed to push the fire engine back into the road and half-attached the chains again.

Sarcasm is always a good leveller and comments like "How lucky – a Land Rover" and "Wouldn't it be useful if we had a Land Rover on this trip?" did the job for some of us. The ice chains worked wonders and soon we were back on the dry plains again and, as we took of the chains, wondered if the moving carpet of zebra and wildebeest around us could ever imagine snow and ice.

Our second cheetah of the trip appeared out of the bushes and we turned off the road to follow him as he looked ready to kill. Predictably the big, red vehicle unfortunately unnerved him and his hunger pangs were the only thing killed on that session, so we returned to the track and continued on our way.

We were not to be so lucky with the filming sadly, and, after several frustrated attempts to capture a long shot through the animals, who kept "Buggering off at the critical moment" (which according to Tim is technical film-making terminology), Graham eventually set up a tripod with some camera-friendly zebra. At the critical moment the shot was ruined by the arrival of a local tourist truck belching fumes and smoke from every orifice which scattered the lot.

"I wish they would have buggered off at the critical moment," muttered John – endorsing Tim's point but not quite under his breath.

And so it was that a sorry film party joined the fire engine for lunch, where even the proximity of a pair of dung beetles burying a wildebeest turd ball wasn't enough to fire their flagging enthusiasm. Graham drove the fire engine after lunch and managed to obscure us in a cloud of dust every time that he slowed down – "The road's fault" – and then Tim had a go at it, accompanied by curious noises from within the depths of the vehicle as he kept insisting that reverse gear was preferable to second gear when slowing down for hazards. Having given up driving and gone back to being a sound man, Tim was then further frustrated during the recording of a wild track of excited humans chatting about seeing vervet monkeys up in the trees.

These beautiful creatures have black faces, fringed with white hair on grey, furry bodies and the males of all species have a pale blue scrotum and a bright red penis. But rather than providing an Attenborough-esque quality to the soundtrack, the conversation degenerated into a discussion about their sky blue bits – which was not language he wanted for the film. The ensuing, and as then unresolved, lively debate about the correct plural for the word scrotum (*scrota*, *scrotum* or *scrotii*) also proved frustratingly inappropriate for his soundtrack.

Without further literary or genealogical discussions, we at last reached our target camp for the night – the edge of Ngorongoro Crater – with only one more filming incident missed.

"What's that huge, wooden elephant doing over there?" asked Jamie, whereupon the elephant moved, but the shutter didn't – the camera was still in its case.

CHAPTER 13

Ngorongoro Crater – poets day in Arusha – the Indian Ocean

Apart from being a slightly strange vehicle for overland travel in Africa, the fire engine was even less appropriate for the Ngorongoro Crater itself, so we hired another Land Rover for the day, which arrived at 7am promptly for us to begin. This being Africa (babe) we finished breakfast in five minutes and set off at 8am with our guide for the day, a highly talkative and knowledgeable man called Peruce – whom we misheard at the introductions and called Bruce for most of the day.

Situated in the south east of the Serengeti, the Ngorongoro Crater is 600 meters deep and 20 kilometres wide at its floor and is home to the most unbelievable array of wildlife you could imagine. "It has even been compared in guidebooks to the Garden of Eden," said Peruce, but to his credit he finished the sentence "Although I am not sure about it." Technically speaking it is a caldera, where the volcano has exploded and collapsed in on itself, but whatever it is or is compared to, it is certainly spectacular from the moment you crest the rim and look into it until you are down on the floor in the thick of it. Our trip was made even more breath-taking by the abeyance of rain.

The sun blazed down as we saw lions two metres away, hippopotamus mating – a surprising reward for waiting an hour just to see one yawn – black rhinoceros and a huge, bull elephant, where Gerry beat most of us to the old joke about them:

"Why do elephants have four feet?" he asked in the style of a music hall comic.

"Because they'd look pretty silly with only six inches," we replied in unison.

We stopped for lunch overlooking the other soda lake in the park, Lake Magadi – or Makat as the *Maasai* call it – both meaning salt. Not content with the abundance of pink flamingos on the lake, Gerry and John shared some of their sandwiches with swooping kites who were dextrously skilful at their raids, having presumably practised on many an unwary tourist over the years.

"We are just not creating enough of a vacuum inside the brakes, Jules," Charlie had told me that morning, to which I think I nodded knowingly. So we had left him under the fire engine sorting out them out – and found still him there when we returned that afternoon. We were happy, having gorged our eyes on exotic animals, and he was happy having sorted things out and been tinkering with mechanical items, so smiles all round as we retired for the night.

After a long and relaxed affair called breakfast the next morning and an even longer wait to pay for our board and lodging at the Ngorongoro Guest House, we set off for the northern Tanzanian city of Arusha and, further on, my first sight of Mount Kilimanjaro.

As we left the park we met a friend of Charlie's called Nigel, who was running a Land Rover tour company in Tanzania. Gerry was slightly put out by the suggestion from Nigel that he had been involved in some form of bestial relationship in Delhi when they had last met, to which he was overheard mumbling something about the woman in question not being that bad. But we had a schedule to keep and could not dawdle gossiping about old times – or so Gerry reminded us.

**

After a quick stop for supplies at a local market, where we stopped for lunch was a classic African scenario – under a large tree surrounded by grass plains – after which Jim whisked the Land Rover and film crew off in a cloud of dust to get to Arusha airport to pick up new supplies of film. Avoiding clearing up after lunch, however, appeared to be their only success as the airport and most of Arusha, was closed that afternoon.

"That's Africa babe" I said. But Jim was less convinced.

"I think it is more likely Poets Day," he mused. "Piss off early, tomorrow is Saturday."

The fire engine had decided to travel at a more sedate pace and meet up with the Land Rover later on and so John Dennis' sunroof provided access for a regular supply of us sun worshippers, basking on the fire engine roof in the newly encountered dry heat. We also reacquainted ourselves with tarmac roads to add to the comfort.

Along the side of the roads to Arusha, the bush occasionally gave way to a few young male *Maasai*, not dressed in their traditional dark red robes, but all in black, with white facial makeup. This denoted recent circumcision and showed a rite of passage when they turned from being children into warriors. Charlie waxed lyrical in Wilbur Smith-type language about how the circumcision and rituals worked, to anguished cries and pained expressions from the male members (no pun intended).

"Anyone heard of the local circumciser round here?" asked Gerry. "He apparently lives off two shillings per day – plus tips!"

"I'd heard that he'd slipped and got the sack," said Wink.

Originally named after the Wa-Arusha, the local people who lived there, the city is a major hub of economic and political activity. However, Jim was in fact probably right in his earlier diagnosis of the situation. Everything appeared to have closed in readiness for the weekend and we were unable to change any money, so we made our way to the rendezvous point at the Tanzanite Hotel.

By some digestive quirk, Charlie accidentally introduced himself to almost all the other guests at the hotel whilst they were eating by producing one of the loudest, echoing, belly burps I have ever heard, so we had to keep a low profile for the rest of the afternoon.

Arusha is an extraordinary location, almost on the southern slopes of the active volcano, Mount Meru, and to the west of Mount Kilimanjaro, a dormant volcano and, at 5,895 metres, the highest mountain in Africa and the highest free standing mountain in the world. Although rich in history and culture, we decided to leave early the next day and drive through in order to reach Dar es Salam that evening.

* * *

At 6am and right on time, the fire engine left the camp, having rudely woken up Graham who was sleeping on its roof, leaving the Land Rover crew from the day before to join us in Dar es Salam having picked up their kit from the airport. We were treated to a magnificent sunrise and some spectacular views of Kilimanjaro as we passed to the south of it.

We experienced the harsh life of a street trader in the town of Moshi, which is on the slopes of Kilimanjaro, where we stopped to change some money. We were down to our last few shillings. Wink spent the last 200 shillings on two packets of cigarettes from a young man who, until that point, had only been offering Jamie singletons. When the transaction was completed, another man who obviously felt that he should have been doing the trade from his stall walked up to our man and punched him in the face.

We then had to wait until 10am for diesel, being told every other minute that "Don worry – him man arrive now" and half expected our pump man to be attacked for nicking business off another garage round the corner. All the traders here seemed to be more intent in arguing with each other, but he wasn't hit by anyone and we eventually set off at a slightly slower pace than tarmac might have implied as the roads were built in sections with large expansion gaps between each one.

Graham and Tim had had a successful, if slow, visit to the airport but had faced a dilemma in the duty free shop – only Embassy or Sportsman ciggies, so they bought half and half, but having tasted the former had traded them for the latter with every boy who tried to sell them a *smoke*. It appeared that Jim had also used his unique navigation skills and taken them on a scenic route to the Kenyan border, but we still entrusted them to go ahead to sort out rooms at the Baha Beach Hotel whilst the fire engine plodded on, eventually arriving at the hotel at 4.30am.

* * *

Having arrived so close to the dawn it seemed a pity to go to bed so we all went swimming in the Indian Ocean and prepared for a couple of days at the seaside. Jamie, Charlie, Jim, Gerry and I mucked around on a piece of cement piping until the local Indian boys joined in rather aggressively and the old phrase two is company, three is a deformity proved true, so we went off for breakfast at about 8am, leaving Jim and Charlie asleep on the beach. Nowadays this is probably an ill-advised thing to do, but in another sign of how things have changed throughout many parts of Africa, it was relatively safe back then.

Over breakfast we decided to rent some windsurfers for Charlie, Gerry and Graham and a Hobi-cat for Jim to get in some sailing. John, Wink, Jamie and I decided that we would go snorkelling on an island just off the coast.

We got to the hire place having had to pay to enter the hotel's grounds, only to find that their catamaran was broken and the windsurfing boards were unusable – the sails looked as though they had been the main course for a moths' banquet. On top of that, the snorkelling was off because "Man with swim stuff not work today!"

Ho hum. Stranded in paradise, the four of us went to the island anyway and had a fantastic day swimming amongst loads of multi-coloured fish, black and spiny sea urchins, eels, a couple of sea snakes and many different types of coral.

Meanwhile, back on the mainland, Gerry had manufactured refunds for the entrance fee and the others had gone back to spend the day in the bar, on the beach, in the bar, on the phone, in the bar, or asleep (in the bar).

Fortunately, but rather unwittingly, we managed to catch the last boat back from the island and arrived just in time to rescue John, Tim and Gerry (who then introduced Wink as his wife) from the amorous attentions of one of the local prostitutes, who had invaded the hotel as it was party night for the locals. After dinner, Sandy, one of the ladies of the night who probably looked better by (snuffed-out) candlelight, took a shine to John and joined us at the bar. "I'm a member of parliament for the Charlie Chaplin Fan Club," she announced proudly, which we probably correctly interpreted as "Take me – I'm yours for ten bucks."

There being safety in numbers, we all chatted to her and she told us about her experiences in England, which appeared to be edited highlights of barely understood snatches of pillow talk accrued during her professional lifetime. She eventually left us after we had all refused to sleep with either her or her friends, or to even buy her a drink. Wink successfully rescued Gerry and Graham from two of Sandy's other friends, by playing the dutiful wife, saying she was jealous of the other women's attentions.

All in all it was a fun evening and we retired to our separate ways still laughing about Sandy's parting story (apparently true but relying heavily on Tim's explanation that it was an old English custom to call drunk men sausage jockeys) about some Swedes who, when one of them fell asleep, she had pulled down his pants and stuck a salami up his bottom.

***

The next day was slightly more energetic for Charlie, Jim, Wink and Graham who went to see if the British Embassy could fix it for the film crew to send some film back in the diplomatic bag. A great idea in principle, but we could have saved them the trip with the answer then and there. However, it gave us the chance to unpack and clean both vehicles before we had a final day of relaxation in preparation for a noon departure the next day.

CHAPTER 14

Accident and emergency

My luck with water supplies had run out and the plumbing was off at the campsite when we came to leave, so it was a quick sprint up the beach with three jerry cans to the film crew's bathroom. The return journey with 60 litres of water was considerably less athletic and more of an undignified shambles back over the sand, but we made it and eventually set off.

After ten minutes on the road, Gerry and Charlie needed to pop into the post office to send a couple of telexes, so we were left to our own devices as tourists in the huge wood and stone carving market, just on the outskirts of town.

"Halve their prices and give no quarter" said Jamie and it proved a successful technique. Before long we were loaded up with some beautiful wood carvings for transport back home, back with Gerry and Charlie and finally leaving Dar es Salarn shortly after 3pm.

There were good tarmac roads ahead and we anticipated making good time with the aim of getting as near as possible to the Zambian border in order to cross the next afternoon. Unfortunately this was not to be as we were shortly about to have our third major crisis on the expedition.

As expected the roads weren't too bad and we had made good time, so by about 7.30pm the fire engine was entering Mikuma National Park when we noticed that the Land Rover was no longer in sight behind us. This not being overly unusual, we crawled along to allow it to catch up, but, having gone at a snail's pace for some 15 minutes with them still not in view, Charlie decided to turn around and go back and find them. We flagged down a lorry driving the other way who told us that a white Land Rover had rolled over about 20 minutes further back along the road. We sped off to the area with dread in our hearts.

The wrecked vehicle was eerily picked out against the darkening night sky by the fire engine's headlights. It was upright, but facing the wrong way and half on and half off the verge on the wrong side of the road. The tarpaulin covering the roof rack on the Land Rover was hanging in shreds and the front roof was staved in down to the dashboard level on the passenger side. All four doors were buckled, the front nearside wing was crushed onto the tyre and the rear offside tyre was flat. There was no sign of either Jim or Jamie. No one was around and the Land Rover's contents, including the seats and spare wheel were missing.

As we were inspecting the damage and noting with even more alarm small traces of blood on the passenger door, some local villagers came up and told us that the occupants had been taken to hospital in Moragora and weren't too badly hurt. Two of the villagers got into the fire engine with Charlie and Gerry to show them the way (and, as it turned out later, to help themselves to Wink's wallet) whilst she and I stayed with the wreckage of the Land Rover, ironically to see that nothing else disappeared from it.

About three hours later, just after 11pm, the fire engine returned with Charlie having seen Jim and Jamie and bearing good news – both were alive.

Jim had a cut eyebrow and a few bruises and Jamie had a very badly grazed back but seemed relatively together. Gerry had elected to stay with Jamie in hospital and to be there the moment the results of his X-Rays came back. Also of positive note was that the back of the fire engine cab was piled high with stuff which had been rescued from the Land Rover by some other locals who, after some initial thieving, had been organised by their village chief to salvage what they could and load it into another Land Rover, which had stopped and which took the injured Jim and Jamie to hospital.

In the light of the fire engine's headlamps, Charlie and I then straightened the torsion bar, which was bent to an almost perfect right angle, by driving over it with the fire engine to the amazement of the locals and the police who were all impressed with Charlie's improvisation. The Chief did ask if it was bent when we first showed it to him, but he got the gist of things as soon as the mad people drove over it on purpose to remove the right angle kink. Having replaced the tyre and winched out the front wing and hammered the roof station up and back outwards we stopped to admire our work.

"Anything else?" asked Charlie.

"No," I replied, "I think the rest looks ok."

"Fuckwit," was his laughing response and his smile broadened even more as the engine started at my first turn of the key.

Optimistically I resolved to drive it into town some 30 kilometres distant, however, 500 meters later I pulled the Land Rover on the verge with another flat tyre. Wink and I elected to stay and guard the remains of the vehicle overnight (it being 3.30am at this stage) and Charlie took the wheel and the spare tyre back with him into town to be mended the next morning.

* * *

We were awakened by various brown faces peering through the holes in the Land Rover and for the first half an hour of the day we became guides around the sorry wreck. Or at least people who pointed to it for most of the vehicles that passed and commented through their windows. "Nice parking" said one.

Then another English Land Rover pulled up and out stepped Bill and Marie-Anne, a couple whom we had met in the market the day before. Having inspected the wreckage they put a brew on which was very welcome and we chatted for about two hours, all of us trying to blot out Bill's first comment as he stopped which was:

"And to think we were really envious of your Land Rover yesterday!"

Charlie and Gerry then arrived and inspected the crash site and together we began to piece things together.

It appeared that they had pulled out to overtake a lorry parked on the inside of a bend and, meeting another truck coming the other way in a compete blind spot, had been forced onto the flat verge the other side. The adverse camber of the verge (i.e. the fact that it appeared to have given way under the weight of a vehicle having become a very steep bank) caused the wheels to catch and jar as they came back onto the road. This had apparently flipped the Land Rover over, and it came to rest on the passenger side after an unspecified number of rolls. Jim had ended up occupying the front passenger's seat and foot well and Jamie, having left the vehicle through the open window at some point during the gymnastics, had ended up lying on his back in the middle of the road having tried to use his body as a brake.

All pretty grim stuff, so we put the wheels on and followed the fire engine back to Morogoro, about 200 kilometres east of Dar es Salaam, with the back wheel wobbling unhappily on its axle. We then spent the afternoon in the garage forecourt assessing the true nature of the damage, Charlie having first amused the locals by driving in and getting out through the windscreen.

We visited Jamie in hospital, who explained his injuries and feelings mainly through a series of grunts and groans, but he did raise a smile when I explained, "And that's what happens when you get out of a car when it is still moving." Gerry sorted out an X-ray and went to find a doctor to interpret the plates and we had even better news, no breakages or internal bruising, just bad, deep grazing.

We then sorted out the salvaged stuff and made a list of missing pieces, which Gerry got officially reported as 'lost in the accident' and we took both vehicles around to a restaurant owned by a woman called Dimtra. She had been visiting a friend in hospital when Jim and Jamie were brought in and had helped them with the language barrier and fed them, extending the hospitality to us as well, by also letting us sleep on her floor.

* * *

Jamie was released from hospital the next day and we took him to the police shack to give his statement, which despite consisting of just the one phrase "I don't remember anything," still took the sergeant most of the morning and a whole side of A4 to write and fully encapsulate for their records. Having competed this and the various legal formalities, we decided to return to Dar es Salaam to regroup and recover our senses.

Jim and I went in the Land Rover with Jim driving "Same principal as falling off a horse," he said, as he got behind the wheel and, once we had donned our disguises as the masked avengers to compensate for the lack of windscreen, and I had crassly said to Jim "Assume crash positions," we set a wheel-wobbling pace for the others to follow.

The fire engine valiantly tried to slow down so as not to overtake and our convoy only paused for road tolls and to pick the odd butterfly, or bug, from our teeth – Jim and I soon knew how a car radiator feels. Despite there being what seemed like a force ten gale blowing through the non-existent windscreen, I managed to fall asleep thus speeding up the journey and making Jim see that I was happy and relaxed for him to drive. Luckily though, he didn't relax enough to follow suit.

***

Back at Baha Beach Hotel we re-joined the film crew, who were celebrating Graham's birthday and they inspected the damage with appreciative raises of the eyebrow despite privately realising that, once again, they had unfortunately missed the action.

CHAPTER 15

Rebuilding the Land Rover – Zambia in a blur – Victoria Falls

Back in Dar es Salaam, we held several post-mortems on how the accident had occurred and Charlie and Gerry took the Land Rover into town to see if it would be possible to continue the trip.

Unfairly sometimes dubbed the armpit of Africa, Dar es Salaam seemed to provide more than enough of what we needed and, having found a garage and Land Rover specialist, the decision was made to remove the roof and create a cabriolet version. This would facilitate 'popping' the doors back out from their jammed positions by inserting a hand-operated car jack between them, and to fully test the vehicle for any stress weaknesses caused by the unorthodox stopping method we had used. They also managed to locate a windscreen mounting on the second day, so things were looking positive for the final leg of the journey.

Jamie and Jim were making good strides on the healing front, with Jim's stitches coming out easily and Jamie using the warm seas to assist in the removal of his dressings to check progress. One of the Australian women staying in the hotel was a nurse who offered to oversee things and there was huge relief from everyone when Jamie's grazes, once uncovered, revealed themselves to have healed amazingly well.

The temporary stop also provided us the opportunity to repack the remains of the supplies and spares from the Land Rover in the fire engine's sin bin, the former central water reservoir which we had converted into our main storage area. While doing this heavy work, Tim and John decided to help mend the rear passenger door on the fire engine which was cracked badly around the frame and had become stuck firm. John's diagnosis was as astute as ever: "You know what's wrong with this, don't you?" he said. "It's broken." Armed with this technical knowledge, we decided to tape it shut rather than attempt to fix it.

***

The Land Rover, fire engine and Jim were recovered enough for a road trip, however, Jamie was still in a lot of pain and sensibly opted for a shorter burst on a flight to Harare, rather than the prolonged intensity of a few days in a car seat. Jim's spirits were much higher now and sharper than for some time as he acerbically demonstrated to a German, who was less than subtle in querying the aptitude of Land Rover to build suitable overland vehicles.

"I don't remember seeing too many Mercedes crossing in the Sahara, mate."

Finally, we were all ready to set off and we bid a temporary farewell to Jamie from the now topless Land Rover complete, with its black and white patchwork of body panels (matching them would have meant many more days of delay). We stayed in view of each other now on roads which were good, as was our pace, only slowing momentarily at the crash site for Jim to see the still clearly visible tracks and gouges left by the roof on the road, and finally clear it out of his memory.

It was then that we began to experience some of the side effects of the work done to the Land Rover once we were just south of Morogoro (again) and inside the Mikumi National Park, Tanzania's fourth largest. We were watching an elephant feeding, barely a couple of metres away from us, in the reflected glow of our headlights. The contribution provided by the Land Rover headlights was decidedly feeble until we applied the handbrake. This electrical fault and some strange wiring not only enabled the handbrake to control the dipswitch, but it also made the temperature gauge show the engine to be overheated and the battery to be flat, so the rest of the trip would at least be curious.

* * *

Feeling greatly refreshed from a three and a half hour sleep we set off at 6.30 am the next morning, with Charlie in a very humane mood and actually slowing down to avoid some chickens and chicks. However, all was back to normal soon as the next poultry pedestrians received the customary "Get out of the bloody way" as he increased the acceleration. It was surprisingly tiring being back on the move, but the roads increasingly improved and the only major delays were roadblocks, which were also escalating in frequency.

At one, a policeman asked Charlie if Jim was his father and was slightly flummoxed when Jim good-naturedly retorted, "Not only would I have been too young to sire Charles. I also hope that I could have done better."

Having gone through what may possibly be the only drive-through banana stall in the world, we stocked up on our natural supplies of potassium (a very good bonding agent for healthy movements) and arrived safely at the border. Coming to a halt, we now plainly saw the benefits of topless Land Rover travel evident on Wink and Jim's faces, which were indecipherable in colour from those of the locals – prompting a hasty rota system for the sun-worshippers.

We stayed the night in a small tourist hotel on the Tanzanian side of the border in Mbeya, a former gold mining town, which is set in what is sometimes referred to as the Scottish highlands of Africa, due to the proliferation of heather and bracken on the surrounding hills.

After the long drive we were not best placed to appreciate our surroundings and, when the hotel's evening entertainment only consisted of a vehemently political lecture from the owner, we turned in early.

***

Having suffered from a lack of tea or coffee the night before due to the fact that there was no water in the hotel, we settled down to breakfast in keen anticipation having not had our orders declined. The pleasure was unfortunately short-lived for the tea drinkers as the water had obviously been previously used to boil corn on the cob, but the eggs were nice, as was the toast when added to our own jam, and so we drove the last 50 metres of Tanzania in high spirits.

Our mood was unchecked as we crossed through both sections in one hour and forty minutes, to the accompaniment of smiles from a welcoming committee from Zambia, who had been informed of our arrival by the Foreign Office. This friendly service was continued at all police checkpoints and we reciprocated by giving a lift to a brother of one of the policemen, although Jim in the Land Rover expressed some doubts to me "If he is his brother then I'm the Pope." Now Jim definitely wasn't His Holiness, but we dropped him off further down the road to warm smiles and handshakes and no family interrogations.

The helpful and co-operative mood was spoiled within the hour when, having decided to pull off the road for a sandwich break we drove into an army road block. The soldiers were most probably bored stiff with their lot in life and proved to be lacking in all co-operative spirit whatsoever and we were soon overrun by them. Swarming all over the fire engine, questioning the taped-up passenger door, looking at our passports and delving into our bags for any goodies which might be of use to them. It was a field day for them and one had a near sexual accident when he discovered Charlie to be carrying $50 more than was declared on his currency declaration form. This was sorted out at great length as the extra cash was proven to be Gerry's, but being kept together as it was in $20 bills, which even the overzealous ferret had to admit was difficult to split $150-$50.

Apart from stopping for a drink in the outskirts of Lusaka, the capital city, that was all we really had to experience of Zambia as we had travelled some 1,200 kilometres that day. After the briefest of overnight rests in an obliging sand scrape, we made further good time and reached the border at Livingstone at noon.

We contacted the film crew, who were already ensconced in Zimbabwe's Victoria Falls Hotel, to let them know of our imminent arrival and we waited on the Zambian side to let them set up for filming. Gerry and I went to check out the falls themselves, taking the precaution of removing our shirts first which proved to be a pointless effort as the spray reached up over 200ft and it was like standing outside in a torrential rainstorm. This was reinforced by a policeman at the guard post, who said that because of the spray, it effectively rained all year round.

"Just like in England," he said with a gleaming smile.

We passed through the border and over to the Victoria Falls Bridge – a spectacular, 198 metre parabolic steel arch almost 130 metres above the lower water mark of the Zambezi River in the gorge below. Originally conceived by Cecil Rhodes, it was manufactured in

England, shipped out for on-site construction and carries pedestrians, road and the only rail link between Zambia and Zimbabwe.

As we were crossing, Jamie met us on bicycle, looking considerably happier and all-the-better for not having made such a long drive across country.

Whilst signing forms at the Zimbabwe post we spied Tim and John going through the other side and after frantic gesticulations we persuaded the Zimbabwean guards to let us re-cross the bridge to be filmed arriving – again.

Charlie's sister, Rachel, came over with us to see the falls from the other side where we met four backpackers who had seen us in Zaire. After two more 'arrivals' over the bridge with Charlie and I in the fire engine, Jamie on his bike, Jim and Wink in the Land Rover and Gerry having problems with customs ("Man, they were just so very slow I almost lost the will to do anything"), we officially passed into Zimbabwe. The shortest of trips (almost round the corner) saw us arrive at the Victoria Falls Hotel where the Zimbabwe Sun Hotel Group, one of the expedition sponsors, had provided us with free rooms.

After a fantastic reception from the hotel doorman, resplendent in a scarlet tailcoat held together with badges from previous visitors, to which we added a Land Rover one, we spent a lazy afternoon waiting for the extensive barbeque, or *braai*, in the evening.

***

Our first day in Zimbabwe was a damp one in all respects, with intense rain, unbelievable amounts of water gushing down over the falls themselves and an update from Vikki on the progress of the film.

She had been through financial hell and back with so many traumas caused by potential financial backers pulling out and a specific helper who had unfortunately created more problems than solutions, but she had held things together fantastically, proved to be as dextrous with financial wizardry as she was good at film making and the documentary was still going ahead.

In the afternoon, the weather eventually abated and we went to film at the falls where we saw spectacular views, rainbows and got absolutely soaked – sound advice from the hotel receptionist: "Wait until the rain stops – much, much wetness now."

Unfortunately for some of the filming the light wasn't strong enough, or, as Vikki put it more technically, "The sun is a bit watery now," but we shot some good footage and we were in a relaxed frame of mind. Particularly Jamie, who commented: "Now that's quintessential England," on looking up contentedly from a colour supplement from home that he was avidly reading. "Er, no," suggested Charlie. "It's Italy, Jamie." The team was back together.

Our rest was unfortunately short lived as we had to press on, so we packed the fire engine and Land Rover with ten people, the financial constraints on the film budget being such that Graham, Tim and John would accompany us on the last section. This added to the problem of having no storage space in the Land Rover, but eventually we were all aboard and we set off down the notoriously dangerous Old Falls Road.

Charlie was naturally extremely apprehensive having not been allowed to use this route since he joined Encounter Overland, a policy taken after six tourists had been attacked by bandits and shot dead about eight years earlier. Still, we followed instructions and kept our eyes open – my school housemaster for some reason always used to say 'ears' in this phrase – and, with Jim ominously informing us that his weapon was in his hand, we made it safely through.

We arrived at what is probably my favourite named place in the world – The Wankie Safari Lodge, which sadly for schoolboys everywhere (and me) this and its beautiful game park has been re-named Hwange. We were treated to lunch and had a swim, all courtesy of the manager Rob, whose quick appraisal of the Land Rover sounded all the more eloquent in his clipped South African accent: "Shit mon – it's really buggered!"

That evening, we arrived at the Bulawayo Sun Hotel (where again the Zimbabwe Sun Hotel Group had provided free accommodation, as they did throughout our stay in Zimbabwe) and we were back on official duty.

We were met by various members of the local Samaritans, who brought along the Chief of the Bulawayo Fire Brigade as a special guest – with his gleaming Dennis fire engine. It rather put us in the shade as, despite being five years older than ours, it was in pristine condition and fully operational.

We spent the rest of the evening with the Samaritans, courtesy of Bowrings who had sponsored the evening and rekindled friendships with several of them whom Charlie, Jim and Jamie had met at one of the many pre-trip fund raising events we had held in Yorkshire. Being the first formal Samaritans event we had attended since Gothenburg in Sweden, it was great to see that the trip had been having such a positive effect on the organisation and we updated them on our adventures, adversities and triumphs.

CHAPTER 16

Ambassadorial duties – arrested by the military – South Africa

Peter and David, two of the Samaritans, arrived at the crack of dawn the next day with the promise of seeing Zimbabwe at its very best and, around 35 kilometres south of Bulawayo at World's View in the Matobo National Park – we did.

Formed over two billion years ago with granite being forced to the surface, this has eroded to produce smooth hills, kopjes strewn with giant boulders and thick vegetation. The smooth rock outcrops gave the area its name in the local Ndebele, where it apparently translates as 'bald heads'. And the views from the summit of Malindidzimu, also known as the 'hill of the spirits', were truly breath-taking, but controversy stalks even this most natural of places.

The graves of Cecil Rhodes – who gave his name to Rhodesia, the former name for Zimbabwe prior to its independence from Britain in 1965 – and several other white settlers buried there are a constant reminder of the past and are perceived by many to be an unwelcome intrusion to what is still considered to be a very sacred place. Avoiding political comment, all I can say here is that Rhodes' comments about the chaotic grandeur of the place were extremely well chosen.

This experience set us up well for a morning session of press interviews back in Bulawayo with local and international media (the latter would not be there today due to political sanctions) and then the fun really began.

After the press conference and media photo session (plus several taken by bemused tourists) we were proudly escorted on our route out of town buy the local fire chief, who wanted to give us a fitting 'Dennis' send off. So we drove out along the main route south out of Bulawayo with sirens and lights blazing on the two fire engines – even being allowed through a red traffic light. We waved goodbye after more photos and stopped at a garage while Jim went back in the Land Rover to pick up Vikki, who had been waiting to call South Africa to set wheels in motion for filming permits.

Almost as soon as Jim had gone out of sight, the Zimbabwean army decided to cause us some intense hassle and an over-eager squad arrived from nowhere, with a power-mad leader and ordered us to remain where we were as we were under military arrest. Our crimc, it appeared, was to have driven past a military base and caused great consternation with our sirens and the sight of our flashing lights. We interpreted the consternation as jealousy – who doesn't get a thrill out of sirens and flashing lights? However, it transpired through some frantic and heated debate that somehow the guards had only seen one fire engine and didn't believe our tales of having been granted permission, or of having a formal escort.

Having established the cause of the trouble, they left us under the armed guard of two of their finest soldiers to go and get reinforcements for a complete search. One of our guards looked decidedly nervous and was probably hoping that no one would notice that he'd forgotten the ammunition clip for his gun.

Three hours, an uncomfortable vehicle and body search, 16 officers from the police, army and military police and several statements each later, they verified our story with the fire chief and we were allowed to press on. Why they hadn't called the fire brigade in the first place was beyond us, but at least we heard an immortal comment from one of the military policemen into his walkie talkie.

"Listen to me," he said to a silent machine. "You had better wake up and come back to me on this one!"

Back on the road and as darkness fell, the heavens opened and Gerry, Tim, Graham and I discovered that a cabriolet of any form was not always the best vehicle for sub-Saharan Africa. The tarpaulin became an impro-vised roof with Tim's boom microphone pole acting as the tent pole, and so it was that, amidst driving rain, flapping canvas and cold, wet clothing, we piled into the Monomatapa Hotel in Harare just after midnight to join the snug and smugly-warm and dry fire engine party.

***

Harare was a relaxed place and we spent the easy day in a media and Samaritan whirl. Vikki picked up the film permits for South Africa and, with the heavens still disgorging the remains of the previous night's deluge, we were met by the local Samaritan representative and taken to an event they had orchestrated.

Having been photographed smiling through the rain and despite constant calls of "just one more, please – but with me this time," we then became the real focus of attention as we recounted our adventures to a captive audience. I like to think it was our tales of excitement and adventure which kept them there for so long, but it was absolutely pouring down outside so that may have helped any decisions not to go home.

Jamie's leg had swollen up by the end of the evening so he retired early to rest up in advance of another day back on the road and ambassadorial duty call in Mutare, while we continued our traveller's tales into the small (and by now dry) hours.

Several years later I revisited Harare and was walking down the street when I spotted a blue overland truck like Critter's overland one in Kisangani. With memories of our fire engine trip rushing back to the front of my mind I strolled up to the cab.

"Anyone know a guy called Critter?" I asked the woman in the passenger seat, when out from under the engine came an oil- and grease-blackened apparition.

"Where's your fire engine, then?" Critter asked.

Not perhaps such a small world, but it seemed so at that moment.

But, back to the next morning and, much to everyone's relief, Jamie's leg was back to its normal size and we were all refreshed and rested, so we bid farewell to Vikki and set off for our next exotic stop. The near-border town of Mutare, known as Umtali until five years earlier, was also called the Zimbabwe's Gateway to the Sea (as it is less than 300 kilometres from the Mozambique port of Beira) was our goal. Along the way and having just crossed over the spectacular Christmas Pass, Jim spotted a suitcase abandoned at the side of the road and realising its potential for our imminent journey home, hopped out of the Land Rover and threw it in the back – perhaps we had been travellers for too long.

From out of the shade of a lean-to in the bush, where he had been happily lazing the day away ran a soldier who chased after Jim and demanded his case back. He had been quite happy leaving the bag where it was until he saw that it had some value to someone: *that's Africa babe*. Having decided that Jim was an obviously dodgy character, the soldier then followed him to a bush to check that there wasn't another suitcase there and that Jim really was going to have a comfort break (as the American's like to call it). Satisfied on both counts we were allowed to progress and arrived without further incident at the Mutare Sun Hotel.

We were met by the local Samaritan representative and spent a few hours in the company of the local crew, outlining our adventures and again passing on the message of goodwill we carried from HRH the Duchess of Kent.

* * *

As a farewell and thank you, the Samaritans presented Wink with a huge bunch of Protea – the feathery bush-like South African flower, sometimes also known as sugarbushes after the Afrikaans name for the flowers, suikerbos – and we set off once more into the rain.

We had used the morning productively and created a Heath Robinson roofing arrangement in the Land Rover with Tim's microphone/tent pole now augmented by clipping the tarpaulin along the top of the windscreen and tied down to the door handles. The only drawback to the arrangement was that we had not only made it rainproof but also escape proof, so it was also a question of fingers crossed for the rain to continue and for no need to evacuate.

Fortunately for those in the Land Rover, no escape plans were needed as the rain was unrelenting. As was our pace and we trucked on into the night and straight through the town of Masvingo (formerly known as Fort Victoria), without even managing to look in on the spectacular ancient ruins of Great Zimbabwe, from which the country took its name following independence.

* * *

Also known as Mzingwane, Beitbridge is the border town and actual bridge which spans the Limpopo River, which was to provide our access point into South Africa. In those days, South Africa was still politically isolated due to its Apartheid policy of racial segregation, and this was a difficult crossing for us, balancing our desires for the trip with our concerns about the regime.

And while we completed the formalities in record time, the border guards became obstreperous when we asked for our visas to be stuck on the plastic part of our passports for easy removal if they caused a problem in future.

"If you are not proud to come to our country then don't come," challenged one of them. But having tested our diplomacy, they relented (in full knowledge of the global realities of our predicament) and then, to their absolute delight, hit upon a bureaucratic hurdle to get their teeth into.

One official became excited over the camera, lenses, sound and general film equipment and demanded a £10,000 bond from us for the documentary paraphernalia. So we were split up into different factions by the guards. Graham and Charlie, politely explaining that a bond of any sort was out of the question; Gerry diplomatically entertaining two guards who were uncomfortably inquisitive about our political views on Apartheid; Wink targeted by second-generation South African who insisted he was actually Scottish; and the rest of us keeping a low profile (on the fire engine roof sunbathing).

So it was certainly no thanks to my efforts that parentage and politics were smoothly resolved and Graham and

Charlie, with written support in the form of trip documentation from the British Foreign Office, finally managed to barter the guards down to nothing – a mere four hours later. And so we entered our 21st and final country with absolutely no local currency whatsoever – trade embargoes meant that the South African rand was only available within the country's borders.

Our first stop, at a bank, was not however successful. All foreign exchange dealings had been suspended for two days until the start of March whilst the exchequer recalibrated its exchange rates – or "Gets its act together," as the bank clerk informed us.

We only needed fifteen minutes to get ours together and, after some gentle group persuasion, we managed to change some money at the old exchange rate and, appropriately armed for shopping (with ready cash), we invaded the nearest Winkle (or supermarket to most people). We then headed off with only sketchy details of where Grania Ogilvie lived, to base ourselves there for the next couple of days.

CHAPTER 17

Final sponsorship commitments – Jim's departure – Cape Agulhas

Despite the directions, off at the third exit and down to the end of a little track-on your right, we found Grania's house with surprising ease and set up camp there for the next two days. Grania was a great hostess, not seeming to mind the fact that we had piles of dirty clothes and she guided us through the maze of Johannesburg and provided the perfect place from which to launch our final assault on the southernmost point of Africa.

We were heroically entertained in town by another of our sponsors, the Hard Rock Café, and spruced up both vehicles with a good spring clean for the final film credits. Unfortunately, having travelled the length of two continents without damage, one of the horns on top of the fire engine caught a branch on Grania's driveway and so we could only play one note of the two traditionally associated with an emergency siren. Other than that, it still looked externally like a respectable Dennis, which some crazed sticker fiend had attacked and covered with corporate logos.

But as we prepared for the final leg of our journey, Jim had to wrestle with his own decisions about home. I believe Jim was feeling honour bound to go back to take over the reins from his stand in back in England, who had already extended the posting by a month due to our delays. However, whatever the issue, Jim had a tough call to make and one which could not have been easy for him when we were that close to our goal, but decided to go back to England. So we waved goodbye to both Grania and Jim and left for the final leg of the journey on the leap year day of 29th February, 1988.

**

The South African *veldt* was breathtakingly open and beautiful and we tore along smooth open roads in spectacular sunlight. Having only two more nights under canvas and now with only eight in the party, three of them being the film crew, it seemed slightly strange to be contemplating the end of the expedition, but as the distance clicked away and the end came in sight, we became fairly contemplative as a group.

On one open stretch of road we realised the enormity of our position when we came across a recently wrecked car – the first vehicle on, or at least near the road, we had seen for several hours. The people by the side thought that we were the rescue vehicles, which being a fire engine and Land Rover was a pretty logical assumption, but after a brief chat we confirmed that they were unin-jured and continued on at their insistence to hurry along the real help coming from the other direction. Charlie mused that it would have been probably better to hitch a lift with us and forget the minimal scrap value, but maybe the sight of our own handiwork on the Land Rover convinced them that they were better off where they were.

In any event, before we knew it, our final goal, Cape Agulhas, was signposted. Named after the Portuguese Cabo das Agulhas, which translates as the Cape of Needles, this is the geographical southern tip of Africa and renowned by generations of sailors as a major hazard and the end of many a ship.

For us it was to be the end of our odyssey and we needed to do it in style so we stopped off in the mainly agricultural town of Bredasdorp, some 35 kilometres north of the Cape and invaded what was apparently the town's only open shop. They must have thought that Christmas had come early as we stocked up on beers, spirits and snack food – the Cape may well be desolate, but we were determined to be dissolute.

And as Gerry pointed out: "You can't go all this way just to get somewhere and not have a wee cocktail or ten to celebrate!" And I have to say, we all agreed.

* * *

As the tires crunched satisfyingly over the pebbled beach under the weight of the fire engine and we crawled to a halt on the shingles amongst the barren rocks at the most southerly tip of Africa, four months to the day after we had set off from London, I felt an amazing sense of achievement.

We had undertaken the trip from the northernmost tip of Europe to the most southerly point of Africa to publicise the Cape-to-Cape fundraising exercise for The Samaritans. The whole effort had been a success in raising a huge amount of money and a great deal of awareness for the charity and this was the moment that it ended.

We had thankfully not had to change a tyre on the fire engine, but three of us had had physically harrowing experiences, we had had two near fatal accidents and we had spent more time in each other's company, than most good friends do in ten years. As a team, we had got on and achieved our goal and although Ched and Jim were not physically with us on this rocky shore, they were mentally there, and so we felt honour bound to be there and go mental for them, so we did.

Cape Agulhas is the official dividing point between the warmer waters of the Indian Ocean and colder ones of the Atlantic Ocean, helping to make the seas well known for strong currents and freak waves (reaching over 30 meters high I have read). But for now they were merely choppy – so Gerry and I naturally decided to go for a swim.

"Which ocean won then?" called Wink, as we stumbled out from the waves and over the stony beach.

I checked down the front of my trunks and it was obvious. "The Atlantic," I replied.

Gerry then became cocktail barman and we mixed up a 'Cape-to-Cape,' the ingredients of which were infused so heavily that no recipe has survived the evening and began toasting those who had made the expedition possible.

Luckily with such a huge project as this (as can be seen from the acknowledgements at the end of this book), there had been many people involved and loads of memories to toast. The closing ceremonies therefore went on through supper and into the small hours before we all camped out strategically for a last night under the stars on a night, which thankfully was rain free.

* * *

Not long after our return to England, I tried to get employment as an advertising copywriter and used the trip and my experiences to try to get noticed.

I had previously applied a couple of years earlier to this specific and very famous agency and had two identical responses back – one from the head of Human Resources and the other from his PA on consecutive dates – saying: "Thank you for your interest in Saatchi and Saatchi, I am afraid we have no applicable jobs available at present, but we'll keep your details on file and will contact you should a suitable opportunity arise.'

Eschewing normal application protocol, I tried to stimulate a more personal approach and wrote:

"I have just driven a fire engine 23,000 miles from the top of Europe to the bottom of Africa, without getting a puncture, and now I'd like to work for Saatchi and Saatchi. Will you give me a chance?"

Although failing to secure gainful employment, the reply had partially achieved the objectives and my letter had at least been read, as I received the following reply:

"Congratulations on your driving skills. Commiserations on your job application ability. No chance!"

Musicology

We provided our own musical soundtrack to the trip and, as you can imagine, with seven different people, we have considerably wide ranging tastes and preferences.

While Steve Smith at Tower Records provided us with may free cassette albums for the journey and five months is a lot of music time, the list below represents the albums which I specifically remember as accompanying us – from which, when I hear songs or see the album cover, conjour up memories from the trip.

Bruce Cockburn	Stealing Fire
Bruce Hornsby	The way it is
Bruce Springsteen	Born in the USA
Chris Rea	Shamrock Diaries
Dire Straits	Brothers in arms
Fleetwood Mac	Tango in the night
Grover Washington Jnr	Winelight
Gerry Rafferty	City to City
Joni Mitchel	Ladies of the canyon
Madonna	True blue
Michael Jackson	Bad
Neil Diamond	Greatest Hits
Paul Simon	Graceland
Pink Floyd	Dark side of the moon

Sting	Nothing like the sun
The Christians	The Christians
The Doors	LA Woman
The Eagles	Greatest Hits
The Proclaimers	This is the story
The Rolling Stones	Beggars Banquet
The Stranglers	No more heroes
Thompson Twins	Into the gap
U2	The unforgettable fire
Various	Now that's what I call music (8)
Queen	A kind of magic

Books

As with music, the books we read were numerous and also proved a valuable commodity for trading with other travellers. Between us we read a small library's worth of books and stories and these are some of those, which like the albums, also evoke specific travel memories for me.

Beryl Markham	West with the Night
Bruce Chatwin	The Song Lines
Desmond Bagley	The Vivero Letter and The Enemy
Dick Bass	Seven Summits
Douglas Adams	The Hitchhiker's Guide to the Galaxy
Harper Lee	To Kill a Mockingbird
Leo Dickinson	Filming the Impossible
Lonely Planet	Africa on a Shoestring
Luke Rinehart	The Dice Man
Michael Crichton	The Andromeda Strain
James Wilkerson	Medicine: For Mountaineering & Other Wilderness Activities
Stephen King	It and Misery
Tom Clancy	The Hunt for Red October
Wilbur Smith	The Leopard Hunts in Darkness

Acknowledgements

I have no illusions about the literary style of this book, or that people will come to it expecting a great epic. It is no such thing, merely my just-over-a-quarter-of-a-century-on reminiscences of an amazing experience that not only shaped my own future and was part of a far greater and more worthy benefit to society.

In recording the events, I have tried to be as faithful as possible to actual facts, but I ask for forgiveness where I have embellished things a little in the telling. However, if there are mistakes that may need correcting, please do let me know via my website www.julianwalker.info and if we are lucky enough to warrant a second run, I will endeavour to make the appropriate corrections for that edition.

One of the many issues I faced when looking back after such a long period of time is the changes that have taken place. Every country through which we travelled (except Zimbabwe, which was partially there but seems to have just had a retrograde step) has had at least one change of government – some democratically and some not. Some countries have also even changed identity (where this has happened, I have used the name current at the time of the expedition). Racial intolerance, ethnic cleansing, coups d'etat, persecution of minorities and systematic abuse of power have all scarred the landscape of the Cape-to-Cape. Many of the places in which we stayed are no longer there as a result of these upheavals and indeed many of the companies and people who supported us no longer exist in the same format or name, although mainly this is for more beneficial and happy reasons.

Time leaves it mark on everything and I have chosen not to reflect these in the narrative but to focus on the moment. The purpose of the whole Cape-to-Cape Project was one of hope and it clearly demonstrated what could be done with perseverance and determination and this book is not meant to be a political statement.

Anything as large as the Cape-to-Cape Project involves a huge amount of people, many different companies, loads of goodwill and enormous helpings of generosity and I would like to say a heartfelt "Thank you" to everyone who helped in any way, shape, or form. Without you, the project would not have been the success it was (and this is also my get out for saying that if I have missed anyone in the lists below, I apologise profusely, and blame the fact that my memory has slipped a little after more than 25 years).

Specifically I would like to thank my wife Wendy, for her patience, sense of humour, support and endurance on this project, Richard Hudgell and the team at Hotcake Marketing in Windsor for their cover artwork, and Camilla Mountain, for her sound advice and counsel.

Most of all, I would like to thank Charlie, Ched, Gerry, Jamie, Jim and Wink, both for putting up with me and with whom I cannot think of a nicer group of people to have spent such a concentrated period of time.

The full list of people and companies to whom the Cape-to-Cape was indebted for their contribution is almost endless, but the following certainly gave above and beyond the call of duty in making the whole project such a success:

A-C

AGFA, Alex da Silva, Allied Dunbar Assurance PLC, Amanda Sabin, Andrew Watt, Andy Cunningham, Andy Leonard, Ann Lewis, Anna Hobson, Anne Walker, Ayeslfords Estate Agents, Bachelors, Baring Securities Ltd, Barlcays Bank PLC, Bartictts, Baxter Fell International, Brasher Leisure Wear Ltd, Brian Gillies, Bulmer Cider, C T Bowrings, Caltex, Carey 'Wink' Ogilvie, Chariot Films, Charles Norwood, Charles & Ginny Calkin, Chelsea Renton, Chemical Bank, Chris Drury, Chris Francis, Christopher Barrass, CIGNA Worldwide Insurance, Clerical Medical and General, Coventry Housing Association, Cresthale Group.

D-F

Daniel J Edelman PR Company, David Bulstrode, David Henriques, David Macbeth, Deloitte Haskins & Sells, Denholme Coates, Denis Specialist Vehicles Ltd, Dennis Bundy, Derek Manser, Derwood, Devon Fire and Rescue Service, Dipre & Sons Ltd, Direct Insurance Service, Document Films, Dominion Insurance, Dr. Chad Varah, E. Boehman, EAS Cargo Airlines, Encounter Overland, Fairways Graphics, Fidelity International, Fred Olsen Line.

G-I

General Foods, Gerry Moffatt, Graham Smith, Grania Ogilvie, Guy Salmon Ltd, Hard Rock Café, Heidi Gordon, Hill Samuel, HRH The Duchess of Kent, Hugo Tudor, Ian Foux, Imatronic, Imogen Pollard, Island View Shipping, No Prints Ltd.

J-L

J H Minet, James Henderson, Jamie Lewis, Jane Lanham, Jane Woodward, Jim Everett, Jo McNally, John Aarvold, John Dennis Coachbuilders Ltd, John Dennis, John Keedwell, John Keenan, Karen McDonald, KLM Royal Dutch Airlines, Land Rover, Legal and General, Lex Service PLC, Louise Foden-Pattinson, Lucinda Prior, Lucinda Thompson, Louisa Henriques.

M-R

Mandy Gough, Maridien Hotels, Mark Sabin, Michael Bucks, Michael Talbot-Ponsonby, Michelin Tyres, Moore Stephens, Murray Johnstone, Neil Wallington, Nelson Hurst & Marsh, Norman Keir, Paul Calkin, Peter Dredge, Peter Griffiths, Rachel Maskey, Rachel Norwood, Rank Hotels, Ray Hill, Richard Bucks, Richard Fox, Richer Sounds Ltd, Robert Bosch Ltd, Robert Ross, Robert Whitrow, Roberston Taylor, Roger Cherrill, Ross Gow, Russell Simpson Ltd.

S-Z

Sale Tilney, Salon Cinecontact, Sea Link, Serena Mytton, Simon Bakewell, SOS International, Southern Sun Hotels, Stuart Davidson, Sue Fern, T.D.K., Tate & Lyle,

Teather & Greenwood, Technicolour, The Cape North Hotel, The Foreign Office, The Owen Agency, Tim Coote, Tim Fraser, Timberland, Tony Woods, Tower Records, Trading Post Ltd, US International Reinsurance; Valerie Packenham-Keady, Vanda Scott, Vikki Hill, Walsh International, Warren Burton, White Water Supplies, Willis Faber & Dumas, Xenons, Zimbabwe Southern Hotels.

END